Christ of the Apocalypse

Christ of the Apocalypse

Dr. C. Paul Willis

Destiny Image Publishers
P.O. Box 310
Shippensburg, PA 17257-0310

"Speaking to the Purposes of God for this Generation"

ISBN 1-56043-104-0

For Worldwide Distribution
Printed in the U.S.A.

Destiny Image books are available through these fine distributors outside the United States:

Christian Growth, Inc.,
Jalan Kilang-Timor, Singapore 0315

Lifestream
Nottingham, England

Rhema Ministries Trading
Randburg, South Africa

Salvation Book Centre
Petaling, Jaya, Malaysia

Successful Christian Living
Capetown, Rep. of South Africa

Vision Resources
Ponsonby, Auckland, New Zealand

WA Buchanan Company
Geebung, Queensland, Australia

Word Alive
Niverville, Manitoba, Canada

Acknowledgments

To author, *Gene Edwards*:
Your recommendation that I change the book from
a commentary about the Christ into a written picture of
Him made the book.

To composer/playwright, *J.T. Adams*:
Your unflinching faith in me as a writer
keeps my spirit high.

To publisher, *Keith Carroll*,
and the editorial staff of Destiny Image:
You turn a manuscript into a book.

To artist, *Tim A. Webster*:
Your brush created the cover
depicting the hand of our Lord holding the seven stars
of the Church above the terror of the Apocalypse.

Dedication

His men in the U.S. Coast Guard called him "the skipper"—this tall man in the navy-blue uniform with the gold stripes on his sleeves. I saluted him when he came "on board" at our house. But then he would lift me to the sky and put his arms around me. Now he is not as tall and his hair has turned white. The navy-blue uniform was put to rest at the end of the Great War when they sent him home. Still, he has the feel of salt water and of a rolling deck about him, and his eyes still speak command. I feel I should stand and salute when I come into his presence. Instead, I put my arms around him and call him by one of the greatest names I know— "Dad"—Cleveland Paul Willis, Sr.

Contents

The Entrance Hall

Welcome to the gallery of the Apocalypse. I am your guide, and it is my pleasure to introduce you to some of the most outstanding and inspired portraits of the Christ painted by the brush of a mere man. First, I want to be sure that you are in the right museum. There are four others, you know!

On the far side of the city is located the gallery of the King. All the paintings preserved there are portraits of Jesus as the Lion of the tribe of Judah. They portray our Lord in His role as the royal heir to the throne of David. They were all painted by his friend, Saint Matthew. The artist shows the lineage of Jesus from the patriarch Abraham, through David, the king, to Jesus—the Christ. You will find that that museum has paintings which compare things on earth to the Kingdom of God.

Just around the corner from the Matthew gallery you will find the museum that contains prints depicting Jesus as the suffering servant. They were all painted by His disciple, Saint Mark.

Mark does not show the bloodline of Jesus as did Matthew. His portraits are those of the sacrificial Lamb. The bloodline of the Lamb is not important—only His perfection. The paintings in the Mark gallery highlight the sinless nature and humility of Jesus.

The next building houses the gallery of the paintings of the physician, Saint Luke. These three museums are clustered together because of the relevance of the paintings they contain.

Luke paints Jesus in His perfect manhood. Thus, he traces the genealogy of Jesus through Mary and back to the first man, Adam. You will find, in Luke's gallery, portraits of Jesus as the seed of a woman, born of a virgin.

Jesus is portrayed as the Son of God. Always submissive. Obedient. You will find, in the Luke gallery, paintings of Jesus being tempted as a man. One painting shows Him sweating blood at the thought of death on the cross.

Midway between those three museums, which are collectively called the "Synoptic Gospels," and this gallery, you will find the magnificent museum of the Trinity.

All the portraits in the museum of the Trinity were painted by the beloved apostle, John. The brush of

Saint John illuminates Jesus as being God Himself. There is a painting of Jesus as the Source of all life. Another portrait shows Him as the Creator of all things. Still another, brilliant in its glory, is filled with the Light of all men.

There is no painting of the genealogy of Jesus in John's gallery. God, who has no beginning and no end, has no genealogy. There is no temptation painting in John's work. God cannot be tempted. You will find no painting depicting the baptism of Jesus. God does not need to repent and be baptized.

In the gallery of John you will find portraits of Jesus as Creator turning water into wine, and of Jesus as the Holy God cleansing His temple. It is John's brush alone that paints the magnificent declaration of the apostle Thomas, "My Lord and my God!"

Were it not for the museum you are about to enter, the other four archives would contain all of man's knowledge of Jesus. The world would have only the apostle John's portraits of Jesus before His incarnation and the synoptic paintings depicting the 33 years of His life on this earth. There are limited sketches that show Jesus after His resurrection from the dead.

The museum of the apocalypse contains several wings that include paintings depicting terrible wars, famines and joyous victory celebrations. In them, you will find paintings of things present and of things to come.

This tour will view only one of the collections in the museum. We will confine our visit to the wing that contains the portraits of the Christ of the Apocalypse. As your guide, I will give you time to examine each painting and then I will interpret what you see. The assessment will be flawed because, like all great art, different facets and diverse meanings appear to each interpreter.

Please do not fail to spend some time in the mezzanine as you leave the gallery. What you see there will increase your knowledge of the paintings you have viewed—immeasurably!

Portrait 1

Lord of the Church[*]

It is as if the canvas is painted with one scene over the other. Waves slap the beach on the island of Patmos. Sea birds soar and swoop in their search for food. The turquoise-blue Aegean Sea stretches empty from horizon to horizon. Yet the artist forms another picture, one framed within the backdrop of the sea.

Fire swirls over the water. On occasion it dances, matching the waves of the sea. At other times the fire twists, as if caught in the whirl of a powerful gale. In the midst of the fire are the feet and legs of a colossus. The giant is so large that the whole of the heavens appears

---

[*]   Rev. 1:12-20.

unable to contain him. In the dark azure of the sky, seven stars orbit within the span of his open hand.

The feet of the colossus glow as brass in the center of a fire. His legs are partly covered by a robe that looks like the ephod of the high priest of old in the tabernacle of Israel. This robe, however, is not girded as one prepared to minister. Instead it hangs loosely, as if the giant is in repose. Also, unlike the linen and gold girdle of the high priest, this gigantic being wears a chest covering of pure shining gold.

The being is standing in the midst of seven gold lampstands. They resemble the lampstand of the Jewish tabernacle. Yet they differ from the lampstand of the tabernacle in that there are seven individual lampstands rather than a single stand with seven lights.

The facial features of the colossus are not visible. The face is filled with a light as intense as the sun. Out of the brilliance, two red eyes send laser-like beams toward the viewer. Where a mouth should be, the artist paints a flashing, bright, two-edged sword.

The top of the giant's head is covered with the white fleece of a lamb. Like glistening snow on a mountain painted against a cobalt-blue sky, the painter has covered the head of the colossus with radiant glory.

The Seven Lampstands

Have you absorbed the magnificence of the colossus? Have you observed the forceful brush strokes? The artist uses bright, bold colors, doesn't he? Notice the use of gold and white to portray the radiant glory! Observe the startling bright red of the eyes!

One thing seems out of place. Everything in the background of the painting—sea, sky, beach, stars—are from nature. Everything except the lampstands. You would expect to find them in a painting of a temple or a cathedral. Why are they central to the seascape?

From Christ Himself comes the interpretation of the seven lampstands. He told John, through the Holy Spirit, that the seven lampstands were the seven churches. That analysis was sent, along with the portrait, to the gallery.

The viewer should note, however, that they are not just seven churches, but *the* seven churches. There were other assemblies of importance besides those named in the book of Revelation. Although the churches located in Asia are independently recognized and separately named in the analysis, (Ephesus, Smyrna, Pergamos, Thyatira, Sardis, Philadelphia and Laodicea), the unity of the Church is indicated by the number *seven*. Seven is an apocalyptic number. The number seven symbolically has another meaning.

The Christ told the artist that the word addressed to the seven churches came from seven Spirits that are before His throne. In the gallery of the Apocalypse there are *seven* churches, *seven* spirits, *seven* seals, *seven* horns and eyes, *seven* trumpets and *seven* vials.

The seventh day of the week is the Sabbath. The seventh day was a significant time in the rituals of Israel. The circumcision of a child was to take place after seven days. An animal had to be seven days old before the Jews could offer it for a sacrifice. Israel had seven feasts of Jehovah, and the feast of Unleavened Bread lasted seven days. The Feast of the Tabernacles was seven days long. The leper was to be purified after a sevenfold sprinkling. There was to be a sevenfold sprinkling of blood on the Day of Atonement. Naaman had to dip himself seven times in the Jordan river to be cleansed of his leprosy.

The number seven is of historical significance in the Bible. After seven days of grace, Noah entered the ark, and the ark then grounded on the mountain of Ararat in the seventh month. The patriarch of Israel, Jacob, worked seven years for his bride Rachel. Joseph interpreted Pharaoh's dream that there would be seven years of plenty and seven years of famine. At Jericho, seven priests blew seven trumpets for seven days, and on the seventh day they marched seven times around the city. Samson had seven locks in his hair as the sign of his covenant with God. It took seven years to build the temple in Jerusalem, and seven days to dedicate it. Elijah prayed seven times for rain, and ascended to Mt. Carmel seven times to look for it.

In the New Testament there are seven words from the cross, seven loaves with seven baskets left over, seven devils, and seven deacons. Jesus told seven parables concerning the Kingdom of God and made seven petitions in the model prayer. James listed seven excellences of wisdom and, according to Peter, there are seven virtues that come from faith.

The number seven, as an apocalyptic symbol, is significant not only as a single number, but also in its multiples and divisions. Seventy times seven is unlimited forgiveness. Seven divided is three and one half, or the imperfect, distressful and disastrous. The judgment through Elijah was three and a half years. The great tribulation period of the end times will also last three and a half years.

The division of seven likewise applies to the seven churches. Of the seven churches, Ephesus, Smyrna and Pergamos stand together. These are the principle cities of Asia. In John's description of the Lord's addresses to the individual churches, there is a marked division between two groups. Three of the churches are separated from the other four. The call, "He that hath an ear," to the first three churches occurs before the word to the overcomer.[1] The call follows the promise to the overcomer in the addresses to the four remaining churches. Seven is a combination of the numbers three, representing the Godhead, and four depicting the world, and indicates completeness. So although the artist's message is to the individual churches, it applies to the entire Church in Heaven and on earth and throughout history.

The Universal Church

When John saw the Church represented by seven lampstands, he saw the Church complete, universal and timeless. However, there are also seven separate lampstands. So there is no single institution that can be called the Church. The message that John submits to the Church is given to local congregations that are collectively called the churches of Asia. Each local church is independent of the others and is responsible to the Lord of the lampstands for its own life and witness. Each local church is to be a light-bearer.

The Son of Man

John immediately recognized that the colossus he had painted through the Spirit—the being standing in the midst of the churches—is the Son of Man!

The title is one Jesus used for Himself. It is a highly symbolic title. The title is given for God in His humanity, in human form. The prophet Isaiah wrote that he saw the Lord sitting upon a throne, high and lifted up, and that His train filled the temple. The colossus John painted has a robe that filled more than the temple—it filled Heaven and earth!

Jesus said, referring to the relationship between Son and Father-God, "He that hath seen Me hath seen the Father."[2] John was seeing the Father-God standing in authority among His churches as Jesus, the Son of Man.

The long, flowing garment indicates His role as Priest-King-Judge. Jesus, in this disposition of time, is related to the Church as her High Priest. He will come again to the earth as the King of Kings and as the final Judge.

The role of Jesus as the Judge is also indicated by the feet of the colossus, which resemble brass being heated in a red-hot fire. Brass is the ancient symbol of judgment. The altars of the tabernacle were all made from brass. All of the instruments used in sacrifice were made of brass. The laver used for cleansing was made from the brass looking glasses of the women. Moses made a brass serpent as a symbol of God's judgment on sin. Jesus on the cross became the brass serpent and took the judgment of the world. Jesus is depicted as the Judge who demands purity of character. He stands in the midst of the lampstands and cries, "Repent."

John explains that to the post-apostolic church (Ephesus) the Lord of the lampstands says, "Thou hast left thy first love...Repent!" To the church worshiping icons and idols (Pergamos) Jesus cries, "Repent!" To the church of the Middle Ages, with her trust in indulgences and works (Thyratira) He cries, "Repent of their deeds!" To the church that claims spiritual life but is in reality spiritually dead (Sardis) Jesus declares, "I will come on thee as a thief, and thou shalt not know what hour I will come upon thee!" To the church in apostasy (Laodicea) the Lord Jesus states, "I will spue thee out of My mouth!"

The Lord of the lampstands does not have His loins girded for action. The golden girdle is upon the breast (heart) of the Christ as a symbol of His affection and understanding for His Church. Christ's last word to the Church is not the great commission, however, it is "Repent!"

The eyes of the colossus Christ are as flaming fire—as red laser beams. His blazing eyes depict the fact that He has omniscience. Although he knows what the real heart of His Church is like and calls for repentance, His eyes of fire are directed toward the world. The author of the Book of Hebrews wrote, "But all things are naked and opened unto the eyes of Him with whom we have to do."[3] The churches are judged where He stands because "judgment must begin at the house of God," but He will judge the world through the Church![4] Peter asks the question, "If His judgment begins in the Church and if the righteous are scarcely saved, what will the judgment of the ungodly be?"[5] The world will not escape those eyes of fire!

The hair of the colossus has the texture of wool and is as white as snow. This colossus is the Ancient of Days that Daniel saw. The white hair indicates Christ's great wisdom and understanding. His thoughts are not like man's thoughts. It is from the purity of His mind that he speaks and His Word is depicted, in the painting, as a two-edged sword.

The Two-Edged Sword

The two-edged sword is the Word of God.[6] This sword is so sharp that it can divide the soul from the spirit as well as separate the thoughts of the mind from the intent of the heart. To those who receive His Word, who believe in their heart and confess faith in the resurrected Lord, there is salvation. There also is, however, an inevitable element of judgment in the Word of God. The Word of God is, as the apostle Paul wrote, "life unto life" or, to those who reject it, "death unto death."[7] It is by the Word that the Lord will reveal the wicked and consume them with the spirit of His mouth. The backslidden church is warned, "Repent; or else I will come unto thee quickly, and will fight against them with the sword of My mouth."[8]

Seven Stars

In the right hand of the awesome colossus, who stands with legs on fire with judgment in the midst of the lampstands, John painted the seven stars which he was told were the "angels" of the seven churches. The Greek word which is translated "angels" can also mean "messengers" or "pastors." John was instructed to write a letter to each of these seven pastors.

Physical letters were not sent to spiritual beings. The stars upheld in the hand of Christ are His messengers! The pastor is as a star, reflecting the glory of the light of the son of God. Jesus, the first Elder of the Church, is the bright and morning star. The pastor is a star sent to guide the church through the trackless dark of uncertainty into the presence of God's glory. The pastor is a heralding star that announces the second coming of Christ, who came the first time as a Savior, and who is coming again in victory and splendor to receive His Bride/Church and rule over His creation. The pastor is an anointed one, held in the hand of authority, strength and power.

The symbolism of the stars being in the hand of the colossus indicate that the pastors are under the protection of their Lord. David refused to do harm to Saul because Saul was the anointed one.[9] The Christ of the Apocalypse holds the anointed ones in His right hand and stands in the midst of the churches. He can remove the candlestick and threatens to do so, but no one comes against His stars without incurring His wrath.

The order of items in which the stars are included is not coincidental. The order is first His voice, then the seven stars, and the two-edged sword last. His voice calls His pastors and His voice follows those whom He has called into the office of pastor with His sword of protection and judgment.

John fell at the feet of Christ as if he were dead, and immediately the Lord placed His right hand upon His servant. The instant John, the pastor of the church, fell, the star-filled hand reached out and John heard the words, "Fear not."[10]

The Lord will judge His Church, but woe to the person brash enough to attempt to pluck a star out of His hand! Whoever is in His right hand is secure, whether star or saint. Who will doubt His ability to keep those whom He has called? Who will challenge this giant colossus, with His head of white silhouetted against the depths of space, His eyes flashing fire, His face like lightning, a two-edged sword for a mouth, standing on brazen legs of fire in the midst of the seven candlesticks?

John fell at His feet as dead. Men will cry out to the mountains, "Fall on us, and hide us from the face of Him."[11] Even satan himself trembles in fear of Him. He is the One who holds the stars in His hand. He is Jesus—the Lord of the Church.

End Notes

1. Rev. 2:29; 3:6,13,22. 2. John 14:9. 3. Heb. 4:13b. 4. I Pet. 4:17. 5. I Pet. 4:17-18. 6. Heb. 4:12. 7. II Cor. 2:16. 8. Rev. 2:16. 9. I Sam. 24:6-22; 26:9-11. 10. Rev. 1:17. 11. Rev. 6:16.

Portrait 2

The High Priest[*]

Star-filled galaxies whirl within an opening in the dimension of time. The painting has a surrealistic feeling about it. It is as if the physical painting has lost its material nature. The vista is one that has never before been seen by any man. Other prophets have given visions of things in Heaven, but this is the first painting of Heaven as seen from Heaven. The painting depicts a sphere of existence in which human weakness and perception has no place; therefore, the painting is unlike anything ever created by man.

In the center of the canvas is what appears to be a gigantic throne. It is no ordinary seat; it resembles what the throne of a great king or emperor should be. A figure

---

[*]   Rev. 4:2-11.

is seated upon this throne. The viewer cannot distinguish the form of the figure, however, because of the brilliance of the light and colors emanating from the being. If the viewer recalls stories of the precious stones found in the ephod of the High Priest of Israel, his impression will be that the one sitting on the throne has a radiating light similar to the brilliance of the ephod. The light is like the jasper stone when it is illuminated and like the deep red hue of the sardius gem when it flashes with internal fire.

Completely circling the throne and the exalted personage is a rainbow. The viewer probably cannot remember ever having seen a rainbow on earth that formed a complete circle or was made of a solid color. Rainbows are normally translucent, and made of light broken into the soft colors of the spectrum of the light. This light in the painting is recognized as a rainbow only because it is in the heavens above the throne and is translucent. But its color is green. It is like an emerald when viewed against light.

Mingled with the jewel-like colors shining from the throne are lightning flashes. One hears thunder rolling with indistinguishable voices. Seven lampstands of fire burn before the throne, and are reflected in the depths of an immense, crystal-like sea.

Four living creatures are portrayed as moving about the throne. They are covered with eyes, not only on their faces, but also over their entire beings. Each creature has six wings and are identical, except for their faces. One has the face of a lion, one is like a calf, one resembles a man, and the fourth has a face like an eagle.

Sitting on thrones located around the base of the exalted throne are 24 men clothed in white robes. Each is crowned with a golden crown.

As the living creatures lead in worshiping the dazzling one who sits upon the center throne, the 24 white-robed men are seen stepping from their thrones and prostrating themselves before the central throne. They are placing their crowns at the feet of the Lord of Heaven.

The 24 Elders

Have you noted the brilliance of the painting? Is it not glorious in every aspect? One does not need light to view it. The painting itself lights the whole gallery! (Well, not the painting—but the brilliant glow coming from the jewel-like glory of the Lord of Heaven.) His glory makes even the perfect circling rainbow seem insignificant!

The interpretation of the portrait of the Lord of Heaven is found in the Bible. The painter assumes that the churches receiving the letters are totally acquainted with the Scriptures. The symbols of the apocalyptic writing are to be understood within the context of other biblical materials. The use of numerals is of utmost importance in understanding John's word paintings.

Twenty-four elders were appointed from the sons of Aaron to offer praise and worship in the temple.[1] There was one high priest and 24 elders who led in the worship. The 24 elders are mentioned six times in the Book of Revelation. Leading the praise before the throne in harp and song seems to be their major function. They have both thrones and crowns to display their royal dignity. Joy in worship is indicated by the elders' harps and songs. Purity of character is indicated by their white robes. Golden vials demonstrate their ministry. The 24 elders/priests represent the saints in Heaven as the redeemed. They are a royal priesthood.[2] Since the picture displays the 24 priests of Aaron as the white-clad elders, where is the high priest with the jeweled ephod?

The ephod was a breastplate worn over the robe of the high priest of Israel. It contained 12 precious stones, the first of which was a sardius and the last a jasper. The sardius stone represented the tribe of Benjamin, which means, "Son of my right hand." The jasper depicted Reuben, whose name means, "Behold a son!" The order of stones is reversed in the painting of the apocalypse because the Church has a high priest who is not from the tribe of Levi, but from the tribe of Judah. He is the first stone and the last stone—the Alpha and Omega!

The High Priest of the Church is not from Aaron, but after the type of Melchisedec.[3] Melchisedec was the king of Salem, and a priest of God to whom Abraham paid tithes. Being a king, the high priest of Melchisedec's order is able to sit on the throne of the Majesty in Heaven and to intercede for the Church. Who is this splendorous being sitting upon the throne? Who shines with the brilliance of the jasper and sardius? The Christ of the Apocalypse! Jesus, the High Priest of the Church!

In the portrait, the royal High Priest sat on a throne that stood in Heaven. The concept of a throne "standing" emphasizes that it is the fixed center of authority. Unlike the temporary and tottering thrones of men, this throne is established. All world governments have a temporary nature. The rule of the royal High Priest, however, lasts forever. The presence of this Priest upon the throne gives assurance that every created thing will give Him obedience. The security of the Christian is based on this fact.

The rainbow, painted as circling the throne, is a sign of God's covenant with the earth.[4] God's mercy completely surrounds His authority. The rainbow is like an emerald in color, indicating that eternal life is found in His covenant and in His mercy. The fact that an emerald bow surrounds the throne indicates that His judgment is always predicated upon His grace.

The significance of the lightning, thunder and voices that are portrayed as coming from the throne can be found in the giving of the law at Sinai.[5] The people were confronted by a mount of fire upon which were thunder, lightning, a thick cloud and a voice of a very loud trumpet. In response to this display, the priests were warned to sanctify themselves. The High Priest of the Church also has a holy priesthood. Paul urged the church at Corinth to cleanse themselves "from all filthiness of the flesh and spirit, perfecting holiness in the fear of God."[6]

Seven Lamps of Fire

John suggested, in his cover letter with the portrait, that the seven lamps of fire burning before the throne were "the seven Spirits of God." Since *seven* indicates perfection, we understand that John is writing about the Holy Spirit and His character.

The prophet Isaiah named seven attributes of the Holy Spirit. He is the Spirit of the Lord; the Spirit of wisdom; the Spirit of understanding; the Spirit of counsel; the Spirit of might; the Spirit of knowledge; and the Spirit of fear (or reverence of the Lord).[7]

The Holy Spirit, as the lamps of fire, is understood as the One who keeps the moral purity of the throne and is a part of its righteous character. The Holy Spirit is not physically visible. His presence is symbolized by the lamps of fire. His being is manifested as being complete through the seven lamps and displayed as pure through the fire. At Pentecost He was revealed in power as the sound of the wind and with authority through cloven tongues of fire.[8]

The Sea of Glass

In front of the throne is a sea of glass that John describes as being "like unto crystal." The artist gives no interpretation of this sea, but refers to it in chapter 15 of the Apocalypse, where it is "mingled with fire," indicating the ordeal from which martyrs emerge, whom John saw standing on this sea. In the portrait of the High Priest, the sea is not related to any character, only to the throne. The sea, therefore, is more likely related to the molten sea within the temple, which was for the sanctification of the priests.[9] The High Priest of the Church is holy and those who come before Him must be justified and washed in the sea of sanctification.[10]

Four Living Creatures

Four living creatures are painted by John as standing in the "midst" and "around" the throne. One of the creatures is like a lion, the second like a calf, the third like a man, and the fourth like an eagle.

Ancient rabbinical writers stated that the four standards for the tribes of Israel that were placed on each side of the tabernacle (where the high priest ministered) were a lion for Judah, an ox for Ephraim, a man for Reuben, and an eagle for Dan. Jesus, the High Priest of the Church, is the royal king-lion, the suffering servant-ox, the son of man and the incarnated deity who came from Heaven like an eagle.

The four creatures have "eyes before and behind," indicating their witness to the Old and to the New Testaments.[11] Jesus was, in type, Melchisedec of the Old Testament, whom the author of Hebrews describes as being "without father, without mother, without descent, having neither beginning of days, nor end of life; but made like unto the Son of God; abideth a priest continually."[12] In the New Testament, Jesus is the High Priest forever.[13]

The creatures each have six wings. This symbolism relates to the seraphim of Isaiah, in chapter 6. Isaiah saw the seraphim, who covered their faces with two wings. This indicated that sight had to be holy before deity. With two other wings they covered their feet, showing that the walk of life had to be holy. With the other two wings they moved rapidly, denoting activity beyond that of normality. The seraphim that Isaiah saw cried, "Holy, holy, holy, is the Lord of hosts: the whole earth is full of His glory."[14] The mercy seat (throne) of God, where the high priest of Israel ministered, was in that place called the Holy of Holies.

The Worship of Heaven

John painted the four creatures and the 24 elders worshiping the One on the throne, who shone as the jasper and sardius stones of the priest's ephod. The 24 elders bow before Him and present their crowns as an offering. How can this One who receives their worship still be their High Priest? The creatures and elders are fulfilling the supreme purpose of the universe. Jesus is the High Priest and "at the name of Jesus every knee should bow, of things in heaven, and things in earth, and things under the earth; and that every tongue should confess that Jesus Christ is Lord, to the glory of God the Father."[15] The High Priest of the Church is the

Lord! Incarnate deity sits on the throne of Heaven. The high priest of Israel is worshiped beneath the mercy seat, the High Priest of the Church sits on the seat (throne), clothed in garments of beauty and holiness, with an emerald of grace circling His glory!

End Notes

1. I Chron. 24:7-18. 2. I Pet. 2:9. 3. Heb. 5:6. 4. Gen. 9:9-17. 5. Ex. 19:16. 6. II Cor. 7:1. 7. Isa. 11:2. 8. Acts 2:1-3. 9. I Kings 7:23-37. 10. I Cor. 6:9-11. 11. Rev. 4:6. 12. Heb. 7:3. 13. Heb. 6:20. 14. Isa. 6:3. 15. Phil. 2:10-11.

Portrait 3

The Lion Who Became a Lamb[*]

The paintings of John continue to portray the splendor of and the events surrounding the throne. Here his brush paints the arm and hand of a man thrusting forth from the brilliance of a jewel-like light. In the hand is a scroll that has writing on both of its sides. The edge of the scroll shows evidence of seven wax seals, such as were used in official documents.

Suddenly another being, separate from the seraphim, appears out of the azure background of the painting. He is man-like and has the appearance of a Greek god. The being is depicted as having great strength.

---

*   Rev. 5:1-14.

There is a luster about this being that makes the viewer realize he is observing a strong angel. A forceful voice seems to come from the powerful angel in the painting. The voice penetrates all of Heaven as the being shouts, "Who is worthy to open the book, and to loose the seals thereof?"

Viewing the painting, we see that the artist is once more caught up in the warp of time and space. John paints the endless vista of Heaven as he reviews the redeemed of the ages in an out-of-time experience. The descendants of Adam flash through the painting. The viewer sees Enoch, the friend of God, and Moses, the lawgiver. John paints Noah, who preserved himself and his family within the ark, and Joshua, who led the children of Israel. Abraham and his sons Isaac and Jacob pass through the canvas—caught in the vortex of time by the painting. The 12 tribes of Israel, from their formation in Jacob to their fall as nations, parade before the viewer. John paints King Saul as well a King David, whom God called a man after His own heart. Ruth the Moabitess and Deborah the judge stand before the moving brush as if time had never separated them. Samuel, with his head covered with wisdom, and Isaiah, clothed in righteousness, are caught in the flow of the brush strokes. Jeremiah, who had cried for godly living, and Ezekiel, who while in the flesh had seen a vision of God's glory, appear in review along with the millions whom John paints, but who are unrecognizable by both artist and viewer.

John then incorporates his fellow Christians, those whom he knew so well during his long ministry, into the painting. Peter, wonderful, strong and so much like a rock, is seen preaching Christ. Paul, keen of intellect and spirit, along with Luke, is seen writing the Scriptures. Mary, the mother of Jesus, is seen ministering in her wonderful motherly way to the saints. John paints the pastors of the churches and with them a vast, unrecognizable multitude.

In the canvas, John paints the portraits of saints who were to come after him. He paints the ages in moments of time! Caught in the painting is the mental brilliance of Tertullian, St. Chrysostom, Augustine and Calvin. The passion of Luther and Wesley is recorded in bold strokes of red. The spiritual fervor of Fox, Bunyan, Whitefield and Finney is captured within the frame. John's brush captures the evangelism of Moody and Graham, along with the mission outreach of Carey and Livingstone?

John also paints those in the hell of judgment, who wait for the everlasting lake of fire. He paints in heinous colors the faces of the Neros, Napoleons, Caesars and Hitlers. The painting depicts multitudes upon multitudes of grotesque bodies rotting in the grave—awaiting the judgment.

Tears from the artist have stained the painting. John did not weep because of the depravity of the sin he saw, or because of the degradation of men, or because of the awesomeness of the judgment. He wept because no one in Heaven, on the earth, or in the regions of the damned was able or worthy to open the scroll.

John hears one of the 24 elders who had been worshiping the Lord of Heaven speak from the painting and say, "Weep not: behold, the Lion of the tribe of [Judah], the Root of David." Now the artist paints what only a spiritual eye can see. There is another being in the midst of the throne. This is not one of the four beasts; this one stands in the center of the four. He is different from the lion-headed beast in that he is like a full-grown regal lion walking in the middle of the fire of glory. The lion is a male in the prime of his strength. His full mane and powerful features have the look that makes men call the lion the "king of the beasts."

As we watch the painting with fascination, the lion's features begin to soften and fade. The mane becomes white and coarse, like the fleece of a sheep. His muzzle flattens and takes on a more rounded, gentle look. His ears become smaller and are more forward on the head. The shoulders become slimmer and the legs thinner, and the body loses its muscular shape. Now it has all of the features of a lamb, except that seven horns rise out of the top of its head and seven eyes look out of its face. Then John paints the form of the lamb beginning to change. Around the crown of its head appear jagged, bloody holes. Its visage is marred with blood. The fleece on its back looks as if it had been skinned. Nail holes appear on the bottom of its legs, as if it has been nailed to a pole to cure the hide. Surely this lamb was dead, yet it still lives!

The living carcass of the lamb is approaching the hand that holds the scroll. He reaches and takes the scroll from the glory of the throne. Immediately John portrays the 24 elders prostrating themselves before the lamb. They have vials filled with incense, which indicate priestly worship. The elders play harps and sing songs of adoration to the lamb. John paints the men and all the beings of Heaven joining in worship. In the painting, all the men and beasts living on the earth join in the worship, and even all things under the earth and in hell bow in obedience. Sounding like the noise of a thousand Niagara Falls, all of Heaven and the universe echo the sounds of praise. A million angels and all of creation shout, *"Worthy is the Lamb!"*

The Scroll

Do you feel as if you have seen a painting of horror? Have we perhaps been in the wrong gallery? Have we been viewing a painting of the holocaust? Or worse? Yes, the painting has its great redeeming qualities, but did the artist have to paint such horror in the background scenes? Did he have to use such dark, foreboding colors? Do the distorted, grotesque shapes and strokes of the brush suggest that our artist is insane? No! John uses such techniques because he is a realist. He is painting a lost world that is quite mad!

The sealed scroll (book) was of particular significance to the artist. It is the sign of a lost inheritance.

When a family in John's time lost their inheritance from poverty caused by crop failure, invasion, business failure, or other circumstances, that loss was written upon a scroll. The scroll was then wrapped and sealed with a wax seal. Around that scroll was added another scroll, written on the outside and on the inside, that told how the piece of property could be redeemed. The outside writing told who the family was who had lost the inheritance, who was eligible to pay the redemption price, and how the property could be reclaimed. Every seven years the scroll was reviewed to see if a kinsman-redeemer could be found who could legally open the scroll. If no one was found, the scroll was sealed again for another seven years. This continued for seven times seven, or until the great day of Jubilee came. On that day a trumpet was sounded, and all of Israel could claim whatever inheritance had been lost. This seven of sevens was called the day of Jubilee or the Day of the Lord.

Jesus stood in the synagogue in Nazareth and read from the scroll of Isaiah:

The Spirit of the Lord is on Me, because He has anointed Me to preach good news to the poor. He has sent Me to proclaim freedom for the prisoners and recovery of sight for the blind, to release the oppressed, to proclaim the year of the Lord's favor.[1]

He then said to them, "This day is this scripture fulfilled in your ears."[2] The Jews in the synagogue understood that Jesus was saying the day of Jubilee was no longer a day in time but a person—Jesus. The Day of the Lord had come because the Kinsman-Redeemer had come!

John painted a scroll that had been sealed seven times. The inheritance had been totally lost. The legacy was all the goodness that God had given, all the gifts of God, all the forgiveness of God, and all of the relationship between man and God. John painted a mighty angel who called for a kinsman-redeemer who can "open the book," but no one could be found in Heaven, earth or hell. No wonder John viewed what he had painted and divulged his heart—"and I wept much." The painting shows that all of God's creation is under the curse of sin. All of God's blessings have been forfeited, and no one has the legal right, the authority, or the power, to open the seals and restore the birthright. It was only after John understood the significance of what had been forfeited and was grieving for that loss, that he was allowed to see and paint the Lion of the tribe of Judah!

The Lion of the Tribe of Judah

Jacob, whose name was changed by God to Israel, called his 12 sons to his bedside before his death. To each son he gave a blessing and a prophecy. To his son Judah, he said:

Judah, your brothers will praise you; your hand will be on the neck of your enemies; your father's sons will bow down to you. You are a lion's cub, O Judah; you return from the prey, my son. Like a lion he crouches and lies down, like a lioness—who dares to rouse him? The scepter will not depart from Judah, nor the ruler's staff from between his feet, until he comes to whom it belongs and the obedience of the nations is his.[3]

The blessing is interpreted to mean that from the tribe of Judah would arise a lawgiver, a ruler. His kingdom would last until the Kingdom of God (*Shiloh* peace) was established, and out of Judah would come the Messiah. His symbol is the lion, for he comes in royalty and strength.[4] Although Saul was king over the tribes, it was David, of the tribe of Judah, who established Jerusalem as the capital of a united monarchy. It was David and his son Solomon who led Israel in her golden years as a kingdom. At the death of Solomon, Israel was divided into the kingdom of Israel and the kingdom of Judah. The kingdom of Judah was destroyed by Nebuchadnezzar of Babylon in 586 B.C., but the hope of a physical kingdom persisted into the time of Jesus.

The disciples asked Jesus, "Wilt Thou at this time restore again the kingdom to Israel?"[5] They were thinking of the physical kingdom promised by the prophets. Jesus indeed promised a kingdom, but not the limited kingdom of David. Jesus is not to be the King of the Jews, but the King of Kings and Lord of Lords of the Kingdom of God.[6] He is of the stock and foundation of

David and of the tribe of Judah, and as such is the Lion of Judah. The lion that John painted, however, is much greater than the title allows. The physical animal, the lion, is called king of the beasts. The physical man, Jesus, is truly the King of the Jews. The spiritual Lord of Heaven, Jesus the Christ, is *The Lion—the Lord of the Universe*!

The Sacrificial Lamb

Surprise! The brush of John turns the portrait into a composite painting. The mane of the lion becomes the fleece of a sacrificial lamb.

The symbol of a sacrificial lamb would be recognized by any schoolboy in ancient Israel. On the day of the passover, every child heard and repeated the story of how Moses instructed the entire nation to take a lamb, kill it, and place its blood upon the doorposts of their houses so the death angel would pass over.[7] Had not Abraham, the father of Israel, gone to sacrifice a lamb when he learned the lesson of substitution, and sacrificed an animal in the place of Isaac?[8] Was not a lamb offered as a trespass offering to make an atonement for sin in the tabernacle?[9] Did not Samuel take a sucking lamb and offer it for a burnt offering to the Lord for Israel, and the Lord heard him?[10] Did not the prophet command a continual offering of a lamb for the nation?[11] The temple had run deep in the blood of lambs offered for the sins of Israel, and John painted "a Lamb as it had been slain."[12]

When John the Baptist first saw Jesus, he cried, "Behold the Lamb of God, which taketh away the sin of the world."[13] Peter said of Jesus,

For you know that it was not with perishable things such as silver or gold that you were redeemed from the empty way of life handed down to you from your forefathers, but with the precious blood of Christ, a lamb without blemish or defect.[14]

The Lamb in John's painting is one killed in the slaughter with the hide and fleece nailed to a post, yet it is alive! The flesh of Jesus was flayed with a whip, and His face was beaten so horrendously that the prophet Isaiah wrote of Him, "His visage was so marred more than any man, and His form more than the sons of men."[15] His head was scarred from the points of long thorns pressed into His scalp. His hands and feet were punctured where He was nailed to the cross. A hideous gash, made by a spear, appeared in His side. The prophet said, "He was wounded for our transgressions, He was bruised for our iniquities: the chastisement of our peace was upon Him; and with His stripes we are healed."[16]

The lamb, in the painting, had been slain—yet it is a living creature! Jesus stood before Thomas, alive, and said, "Reach hither thy finger, and behold My hands; and reach hither thy hand, and thrust it into My side: and be not faithless, but believing."[17] Jesus had been flayed alive, wounded, nailed to a cross like the fleece of a dead lamb, and hung out to dry. He had been taken down from the cross, shrouded in death wrappings, and buried in a tomb. Now the tortured carcass stands alive and says, "Behold." Yes! "Behold the Lamb!"

The lamb of John's brush is not a weak lamb; it has "seven horns and seven eyes." A horn was used to anoint kings.[18] The horn was a symbol of power and authority.[19] This is a lamb of authority and power! The lamb has "seven" horns; therefore, this lamb has complete command and strength. He looks like a lion turned into a lamb, but He is the authority of a lamb turned into a lion! His seven eyes are "the seven Spirits of God sent forth into all the earth." He is omniscient and nothing is hidden from His sight. The slain lamb is God, Himself!

The New Song

John paints the seventh sealed scroll of the forfeited inheritance of mankind as being inscribed on the outside with the qualifications of the redeemer and the price to be paid for redemption. God had said that the penalty of sin was death.[20] Without the shedding of blood, there could be no remission of sin.[21] Yet not any blood would do. It had to be blood pure from the sins of mankind. It had to be blood untouched by the curse of disobedience. The blood of sacrifice, even the enormous sacrifices of the temple, was not suitable because the blood was not pure from the curse. Only One born of a virgin, separated from the sins of Adam, born of the pure Spirit of God, with blood untainted by sin, could be the Redeemer of man's lost inheritance. The 24 elders/priests waited for a kinsman-redeemer. They had in their vials the prayers of the saints that could not be answered until the seals were broken. The four creatures who wait before the throne could not witness God's grace until the seals were broken. The High Priest upon the throne waits. He cannot intercede for rejected humanity until a proper offering presents himself. The blood had to be presented and applied to the mercy seat.

Miracle of miracles, the High Priest presents the offering to Himself, for the High Priest Himself becomes the Lamb to be offered. The High Priest's blood is pure; He was born of the virgin Mary. The High Priest is holy; He has never tasted sin. The High Priest is of the tribe of Judah. The High Priest is of a royal priesthood. The High Priest is the Lion of the tribe of Judah who becomes the Lamb and offers Himself as the Kinsman-Redeemer.

Something that had never before been seen in all of creation now exists. The High Priest, the royal Lion and the sacrificial Lamb are one. The High Priest can minister in the heavens and offer His own blood as the Mediator of a new testament. He can establish, as the Lion, the Kingdom of God.[22] This new reality demands a new song; the song of the elders/priests:

And they sang a new song: "You are worthy to take the scroll and to open its seals, because

You were slain, and with Your blood You purchased men for God from every tribe and language and people and nation. You have made them to be a kingdom and priests to serve our God, and they will reign on the earth."[23]

Ten thousand times ten thousand and thousands of thousands of angels are portrayed singing the chorus, and they sing *Worthy is the Lamb!*"

End Notes

1. Luke 4:18-19 (NIV). 2. Luke 4:21. 3. Gen. 49:8-10 (NIV). 4. Judg. 14:18. 5. Acts 1:6. 6. Rev. 19:16. 7. Ex. 12:3-27. 8. Gen. 22:7. 9. Lev. 5:6. 10. I Sam. 7:9. 11. Ezek. 46:15. 12. Rev. 5:6. 13. John 1:29. 14. 1 Pet. 1:18-19 (NIV). 15. Isa. 52:14. 16. Isa. 53:5. 17. John 20:27. 18. I Sam. 16:13. 19. Deut. 33:17. 20. Gen. 2:17; Rom. 6:23. 21.Heb. 9:22. 22. Heb. 9:11-28. 23. Rev. 5:9-10 (NIV).

Portrait 4

Jesus the Mighty Angel[*]

This painting depicts events occurring on earth that John observes from a heavenly perspective. From the perception of Heaven, he paints an enormous presence descending from a throne. The being is clothed from his shoulders to his legs with a radiant cloud. His face is as brilliant as the sun at midday, and a rainbow circles his head like a crown of glory. He is so immense in size that he places one of his feet, which is like a pillar of fire, upon the sea and the other upon the earth. His enormous hand contains a scroll much smaller than the seven-sealed one John had already painted. This scroll contains ths history of man's sin and God's word of

---

[*]   Rev. 10:1-11.

redemption. It is not sealed. The Being roars with a tumultuous voice, as if he were a great lion. At the sound of his voice, seven other voices are depicted as thundering out of the clouds. At the sound of the seven thunders, the stupendous being lifts his hand into the heavens and swears that time should be no more.

The Angel of the Lord

Is the figure in this portrait familiar? John had painted the towering presence earlier in his visions of the Apocalypse and had named him "another angel."[1] John had been so fascinated with the events surrounding the angel in his other portrait that he had not painted the being in detail. This same angel had been seen standing at the altar of the tabernacle. Now the angel has a golden censer in his hand which he fills with fire from the altar. The strong angel had thrown fire upon the earth before, and John had heard the same thunders, but this time they are accompanied by lightning and an earthquake.[2]

The concept that the angel is the Christ is not foreign to the Old Testament. The "Angel of the Lord" appears throughout Old Testament Scriptures. The Angel of the Lord spoke to the children of Israel as God Himself, in a self-manifestation.[3] Ezekiel saw him in the midst of four living creatures, who had the same faces John saw: the faces of a man, lion, ox and eagle.[4] Ezekiel's angel, like the strong angel of John's vision, was seen in the midst of the throne. His legs were of the "appearance of fire" and there was the "appearance of the bow that is in the cloud in the day of rain."[5]

Ezekiel, like John, fell upon his face when he heard the voice.[6] Daniel saw the angel and said that his face was like "lightning," his eyes were like flaming torches, and his feet were like brass. When Daniel heard the angel's voice he, like John, found himself with his face "toward the ground" and "no strength" remained in him.[7] The resemblance between the visions of Ezekiel, Daniel and John is striking.

Jesus is the Word, or the *Logos,* in Greek.[8] As the *Logos,* He was the Creator.[9] He therefore existed before His birth in Bethlehem as the pre-incarnate *Logos.* From the time of Justin, the figure of the "Angel of the Lord" has been regarded as the pre-incarnate *Logos.*

When the Angel of the Lord, or *Logos,* spoke to Hagar, He called to her from Heaven.[10] The same Word came to Abraham from Heaven.[11] The Angel of the Lord spoke to Jacob and identified Himself as "the God of Bethel."[12] After wrestling with the Angel of the Lord, Jacob said, "I have seen God face to face."[13] As the Angel of the Lord, Jesus spoke to Moses in the burning bush and called Himself the "God of Abraham, the God of Isaac, and the God of Jacob."[14] As the Angel of the Lord, Jesus guided Israel from Egypt.[15] As the Angel of the Lord, He commanded the destroying angel to stop a plague in the time of David.[16] Only One with the authority of God could command angels, bless Abraham, and present Himself as God to Moses.

The different angel seen by John in Revelation 8 could be no other than Jesus as the Angel of the Lord.

No mere angel could have stood at the altar of incense with a golden censer in his hand. Jesus is the Mediator of the New Testament, which the golden censer foreshadowed.[17] Also, God led the children of Israel by a cloud. Clouds received Jesus up to glory. When Jesus comes again, He will come in the clouds and this "different angel" is clothed with clouds as a sign of His glory. The covenant rainbow of God circles His head also. This is the same rainbow glimpsed by John and recorded in chapter 4 of the Apocalypse. In this painting the rainbow appears variegated, where before it was green. The rainbow is the sign of divinity and of God's mercy. The face of the angel is as the sun, and His feet like pillars of fire. This description is the same as the Christ of the Apocalypse found in chapter 1. The brilliance of His visage is an expression of His glory, and the burning feet upon the sea and upon the land are descriptions of His judicial action on the Gentiles and on the Jews. The Angel of the Lord is the *Logos*, the incarnate Word who is the pre-incarnate Jesus.

The Open Little Book

In chapter 5 of the Apocalypse, the Lamb receives a seven-sealed book which, in Greek, is called a *biblion*. The book held by the angel is called, in Greek, a *biblaridion*. This is a diminutive form of the word that emphasizes the fact that the scroll was small. In the next painting the Lamb takes the seven-sealed scroll and opens it, revealing the lost inheritance of mankind and the price of redemption, but in this picture the small book is already open. Seven thunders articulate when the strong angel speaks. John, however, is told not to write what he has heard, and to seal the words. This sealing of the words has a parallel in the Scriptures. Daniel was told to seal a book concerning the time of the end of the ages.[18] This angel also makes an announcement concerning the end of the age. That both sealed messages have the context of the secret timing of the close of the age cannot be a coincidence. When Jesus was in the world, He was asked when He would restore the kingdom. He answered, "It is not for you to know the times or the seasons, which the Father hath put in His own power."[19] The open book and the sealed message of the seven thunders deal with the same thing. The Word concerning God's purpose for the end of the age is a small open book in time; when the events will occur is sealed to all but the angel.

John was told, in his instructions, to take and eat the little book, and that it would be sweet as honey in his mouth but bitter in his belly.[20] John obeyed and found the word he received about the book to be true. As soon as the word was on the inside, John was told that he "must prophesy again before many peoples, and nations, and tongues, and kings."[21]

Ezekiel also was told to eat a scroll and found the book to be sweet like honey.[22] The inside of Ezekiel's book, like John's, was written with "lamentations, and mourning, and woe" and as a result he ministered in "bitterness."[23] The prophet Jeremiah wrote, "Thy words were found, and I did eat them; and Thy word was unto me the joy and rejoicing of mine heart."[24] Then he added, "Thou hast filled me with indignation. Why is my pain perpetual, and my wound incurable, which refuseth to be healed?"[25]

John, Ezekiel and Jeremiah experienced somewhat the same thing. The Word of God is sweet, in that it is a word of grace and promise. The Word of God is also a two-edged sword. As sweet as it is to the saint, it is bitter to the sinner. John is a saint, but since he must prophesy before a multitude of many peoples concerning the end of time and the final judgment, the word is bitter on the inside of him. The second coming of Jesus Christ and the final judgment of the age is a paradox to the minister. He looks forward with hope to the second coming of Christ, but also with the sure knowledge that the event will seal the judgment upon some who have received his word. Sweet in the mouth and bitter in the belly, indeed!

The Golden Censer

The golden censer of incense that is filled with fire from the altar in this painting and the feet of fire placed on the sea and on the earth have the same meaning.[26] Although the "angel" has a rainbow of grace about His head, His burning coals of fire and His burning feet indicate that He comes as an envoy of divine judgment. His judgment comes in response to the cries and prayers of His people; thus, the fire comes from the incense of the High Priest. His feet rest upon the sea (in the Apocalypse the sea symbolizes the gentile nations) and upon the earth (the nations who have been entrusted with the government of God) alike. Living in Israel or in a so-called Christian nation will not help a person when the "angel" brings His judgment of fire. Like the book with its paradox of sweetness and bitterness, the angel brings the paradox of a rainbow and judgment. Having rejected the word of grace, the world must receive the word of judgment. Having been a Christianized nation is not enough. Both they who received the word and neglected it, and they who received the word and rejected it, find themselves under the fire from the golden censer and under the feet of brass. Judgment for supposed good (gold) or judgment for sin (brass) will be no different! To reject the "angel" (Christ) is to be judged by the Angel. There is no escape from the Christ of the Apocalypse's feet of fire!

End Notes

1. Rev. 8:3. **2.** Rev. 8:3-5. **3.** Judg. 2:1. **4.** Ezek. 1:10. **5.** Ezek. 1:26-28. **6.** Ezek. 1:28. **7.** Dan. 10:5-9. **8.** John 1:1. **9.** John 1:3. **10.** Gen. 21:17. **11.** Gen. 22:11,15. **12.** Gen. 31:11-13. **13.** Gen. 32:24-32. **14.** Ex. 3:6. **15.** Ex. 13:21 or Ex. 14:19. **16.** I Chron. 21:15-27. **17.** Heb. 9:2-15. **18.** Dan. 12:4. **19.** Acts 1:7. **20.** Rev. 10:8-10. **21.** Rev. 10:11. **22.** Ezek. 2:9-3:3. **23.** Ezek. 2:10; Ezek. 3:14. **24.** Jer. 15:16. **25.** Jer. 15:17-18. **26.** Rev. 8:3-5.

Portrait 5

The Man Child*

John's next painting draws our attention away from the throne and the events surrounding it, to the darkness of space. A portrait is painted against the eternal pitch-black of the outer reaches of the universe. Against this void John fills the canvas with the graceful form of a woman. She is wearing a brilliant, flowing gown made of the light of the sun itself. She is standing upon the moon as if it were a pedestal in space. A wreath of 12 stars lies upon her head.

The viewer can tell from the shape of the gown, clinging to the mid-portion of her body, that the woman is heavy with child. This fact seems to add to her grace and beauty. The woman's countenance, however,

---

*   Rev. 12:1-17.

shows that she is in the anguish of travail of labor and birth. As John places the image of the woman upon the canvas, another picture begins to form, from his brush, in the unilluminated blackness of the void.

Bright red paint—the color of fire—forms the shape of a dragon-like creature. This fearful monstrosity has seven heads of fire weaving from the single trunk of its body. Each head is encircled with golden diadems, and pertruding out from the seven heads are ten horns. The brush then paints a gigantic tail whipping through the universe. A third of all the stars in the cosmos are caught in the suction of the tail, and hurled with incredible force to the earth.

As the painter moves the brush, he is mesmerized by what he is painting. From the sun-dressed woman, he paints a child born out of the radiance of her thighs. The child, however, is not a normal baby. The brush reveals that she has given birth to a mature man. The man child depicted is dressed in royal garments, is crowned with many crowns, and holds in his hand a scepter of iron. The painting shows a progression. The man child pauses for a brief period of time, and then is caught away from the basic scene into an area of the painting that represents the third heaven.

Like a curtain opening on the act of a play, the brush moves on to the next episode on the canvas, which reveals a war in Heaven. A lustrous archangel of great size and strength leads winged angels to attack the fiery red dragon. A furious battle is illustrated. It seems, to the viewer, that all of the universe will be torn asunder by the fierceness of the battle coming from John's brush. No part of God's creation seems to be spared the indignity of the conflict. Finally, however, the viewer is shown that the dragon and his demons are cast out of the heavenly realm and sent crashing to the earth.

On the next section of the canvas John paints the sun-clad woman as having left her starry realm and gone to earth herself. The dragon, not able to prevail against the heavenly forces, begins to brutalize the woman. Angelic forces, recognizing the woman's danger, supply the woman with great wings that help her fly from the dragon's harassment. Suddenly, out of the mouth of the dragon, John draws a flood of water spewing forth in an attempt to entrap the woman. The brush then opens a great hole in the earth. The water is forced to pour into the hole and is kept from obliterating the woman. The dragon, recognizing that he can no longer destroy the man child, who is safely out of his reach, or attack the sun-clad woman, who has received the protection of the earth, begins to search for the sun-clad woman's other children. The artist, realizing that the dragon is looking for those who did not have heavenly or earthly protection so he can make war on them, lifts his brush from the painting and ends the portrait.

The Sun-Clad Woman

Did you get caught up in the action? Only the Spirit of God could make an inanimate piece of canvas and paint come to life. The brush did not move by John's hand alone. No, this is a work of the Holy Spirit and it will take insight from the Spirit to understand the portrait!

The key to identifying the man child whom John painted is the sun-clad woman. Joseph, the most loved of all of Israel's children, had a dream.[1] In his dream Joseph saw the sun, moon and eleven stars giving obeisance to him. When Joseph shared the dream with his family, they interpreted it as meaning that Israel, (the sun), Joseph's mother (the moon), and his eleven brothers (the eleven stars), were being told that they would have to submit to Joseph. Israel asked, "Shall I and thy mother and thy brethren indeed come to bow down ourselves to thee to the earth?"[2]

Because of their extreme envy, his brothers sold Joseph into slavery. Slave traders sold Joseph to Potiphar, an Egyptian officer in the guard of Pharaoh. At first Joseph did well as Potiphar's slave, and worked into a place of trust until he attracted the lust of Potiphar's wife. Joseph successfully avoided the advances of the woman, but was accused nevertheless. As a result, he found himself consigned to an Egyptian prison.

There seemed no remote way in which Joseph's dream could be realized. Joseph, however, soon gained a reputation in prison as an interpreter of dreams. This fact came to the knowledge of Pharaoh, who had been tormented by strange and repeated dreams. Joseph was brought to Pharaoh, and he warned the ruler that there would be a seven-year time of plenty followed by seven years of famine in the land of Egypt. Joseph advised the Pharaoh to appoint a man over the storage of food in Egypt, and to have him collect supplies in the good years and dispense it to the people in the coming years of famine. Pharaoh responded by appointing Joseph as second-in-command of all of Egypt to carry out the plan. The time of plenty came, and then the time of famine followed, exactly as Joseph predicted.

During the time of drought, Israel sent his sons, with the exception of Joseph's younger brother Benjamin, to Egypt to buy grain. The nine brothers bowed before Joseph, not knowing who he was. But Joseph called them spies and held Simeon as hostage, demanding that they bring Benjamin if they wanted further help. When the famine continued, Israel reluctantly sent his sons, including Benjamin, to Egypt. After Joseph saw the heart of his brothers, that they were willing to die or go to prison for Benjamin and that they had repented for what they had done to him, he revealed who he was. Word was sent back to Israel that Joseph was alive and that he and all the families could have sanction and provision in Egypt. Israel and all his tribes came to Egypt and there they honored Joseph as second-in-command of all of the nation, fulfilling the ancient dream.

The nation of Israel was regarded by God as being His wife.[3] The 12 stars in the crown of the sun-clad woman represent the 12 tribes of Israel. The moon/ pedestal represents her exalted position among the nations. The sun/gown is the glory God gave to her as a witness to the nations. The man child she is travailing to produce is the Messiah.

The Fiery Dragon

John's guideline to the Apocalypse leaves us in no doubt as to the character portrayed in the image of the fiery dragon. He is "that old serpent, called the devil, and satan."[4] Before time, satan was called lucifer and was the "anointed cherub." The prophet Isaiah wrote of him:

How you have fallen from heaven, O morning star, son of the dawn! You have been cast down to the earth, you who once laid low the nations! You said in your heart, "I will ascend to heaven; I will raise my throne above the stars of God; I will sit enthroned on the mount of assembly, on the utmost heights of the sacred mountain. I will ascend above the tops of the clouds; I will make myself like the Most High." But you are brought down to the grave, to the depths of the pit.[5]

The prophet Ezekiel wrote:

You were in Eden, the garden of God; every precious stone adorned you: ruby, topaz and emerald, chrysolite, onyx and jasper, sapphire,

*turquoise and beryl. Your settings and mount-
ings were made of gold; on the day you were
created they were prepared. You were anointed as a guardian cherub, for so I ordained
you. You were on the holy mount of God; you
walked among the fiery stones. You were
blameless in your ways from the day you were
created till wickedness was found in you.*[6]

Neither Isaiah nor Ezekiel could have been writing
about an earthly king alone, although they make ap-
plication to the king of Tyre. No ruler on earth, no mat-
ter how great, could have been in "the garden of God"
or "fallen from heaven." Lucifer was the created,
anointed angel of God, who rebelled and became satan
(the adversary). He is connected to the governments of
the satanic world system, of which Tyre and ancient
Babylon were a representative part.[7] The seven heads
of the dragon delineate the seven world empire systems projected by Daniel.[8] The ten horns of the dragon
are the governmental systems that produce the "little
horn" of the antichrist who, as Jesus was the incarnation of the Father, will be the incarnation of lucifer.[9] In
satan's apostasy, he drew one-third of the celestial creatures with him, making him the "tempter." These celestial creatures are the stars that John saw caught in the
tail of the dragon, now demons found in the earth.[10]
Satan continues to reign as the "god of this world," and
the Church, with God's angels, continues to battle him
even after his judgment was settled through the cross
of Christ.[11]

The Dragon's Persecution of the Jews

Satan hates Israel! The dragon was defeated in his attempt to overthrow the throne of God. He knows, therefore, that he will never "exalt [his] throne above the stars of God."[12] Knowing that, after his defeat in the heavenlies, he could not vanquish God, he turned his wrath on God's special love—God's wife (Israel). Lucifer was told as the serpent, in the garden of Eden, that the seed of a woman would bruise his head. The "seed of a woman" meant that the father had to be God. Who but God's wife could give Him a child? Satan's attack on Israel has been furious!

The power behind the Pharaoh of Egypt, which made Israel a slave nation and commanded that every son born to the Jews be drowned in the river, was satan.[13] He was attempting to destroy the seed! The force behind Israel's trials in the wilderness was satan. The agent directing the defeat of Israel at Ai was the devil.[14] Lucifer raised up, one after the other, the Mesopotamians, Moabites, Ammonites, Amalekites, Canaanites, Midianites and Philistines to oppress Israel for 111 years during the time of the judges.

The strength behind the giant Goliath, who attempted to kill young David before he established the kingdom, was satan. Shalmaneser I and Tiglath-pileser I of Assyria were influenced by lucifer to destroy the Jews, by inspiring terror in their captivity of Israel. The Assyrians skinned Jewish prisoners alive, and cut off their hands, feet, noses, ears and tongues. They also marked the progress of their victories by making mounds of the human skulls of the Jews. Nebuchadnezzar of Babylon carried Jews into captivity, stripped Israel of the temple treasures, burned Jerusalem, and plucked out the eyes of king Zedekiah of Judah. The Jews came close to total annihilation during the reign of Xerxes of Persia, and were saved only through the intervention of Queen Esther.

Alexander the Great of Greece invaded Palestine in 332 B.C., which was reconquered by Antiochus the Great in 198 B.C. and given back to the kings of Syria. Antiochus Epiphanes was made so violent by satan that he offered a sow on the altar of God, erected an altar to Jupiter, prohibited temple worship, forbade circumcision, sold thousands of Jewish families into slavery, used every conceivable torture to force Jews to renounce their God, and destroyed all copies of Scripture that could be found.

In 63 B.C. Pompey of Rome conquered Palestine. The Romans appointed Antipater, a descendent of Esau, as ruler of Judea. Antipater's son, Herod, was so controlled by satan that he ordered all the little children of Bethlehem killed, in an attempt to kill the promised Man Child.

In modern history, who can doubt that the holocaust under Adolph Hitler was inspired by satan? With the reformation of the nation of Israel, satan has ignited the offspring of Ishmael, the descendants of the Egyptians, Assyrians, Babylonians and Persians, to attempt to annihilate the Jew from the face of the earth. This is the great "flood" that the serpent spewed out of his mouth in an attempt to have the sun-clad woman destroyed; however, the "earth helped the woman."[15] The earth that swallows the flood in John's revelation is the governments of the world.

In 1918, the League of Nations gave the right of existence to the nation of Israel. The United States supported Israel with military hardware to help her keep her enemies at bay. In 1990, the United Nations gave sanction to use military means to blockade Iraq (Persia) in her military bid to lead the Arab nations in a holy war to destroy the Jews. Iraq responded with threats to destroy Israel with a biological missile attack. The United States, during the United Nations' "Operation Desert Storm," sent Patriot missiles, and crews to protect Israel. The United Nations had other reasons for releasing "Operation Desert Storm," but God was using them to protect the sun-dressed woman from destruction by the dragon. Satan is "wroth" with the sun-clad woman and continues to make war with the remnant of her seed.[16]

The Son Man

John writes in the guidelines that the sun-clad woman gave birth to a *whyos arren,* which literally means a "son-man." The designation *arren* is separate from *artiginneetos* (a newborn babe) and *arseen* (male). This "man child" is *arren* (Man—Second Adam) and *whyos* (Son—of God). Jesus Christ is the Man Child!

He is called a "child" because He was born to Israel through the house of David. Mary, the mother of Jesus, was of the lineage of David, and thus of the royal line of Israel.[17] In His human nature, Jesus was like every other child born in Israel in His period of time. There was nothing that would distinguish Him as being divine. He was suckled by Mary and disciplined by His stepfather, Joseph. He had to grow, both in body and mind.[18] He played in the dusty streets of Nazareth and worked in Joseph's carpenter shop as an apprentice.

As the "Son," He debated and taught the doctors of religion when He was only a child 12 years of age.[19] The spirit of the child was the *logos,* who was the very knowledge (Word) of God that created the universe. As the Son, He was the Second Adam, who had dominion over creation. As the Child, He was the Son whom satan attempted to destroy by having all of the babies in Bethlehem put to death.[20] At His word, water turned to wine, the wind stopped blowing, and the sea became calm.[21] As the Son, anointed by the Holy Spirit, He drove satan away from His presence with the power of His Word.[22]

The Apocalypse does not portray the 33 years of the life of Jesus of Nazareth on this earth. John's picture of the Man Child reveals only His coming to earth and His ascension into Heaven. The churches, to whom the

Apocalypse was addressed, understood the life of Jesus. As John had previously written, the apostles had heard, seen, looked upon and handled the Word of life.[23] To the Church, the years of Jesus' life on earth were vastly important. To the sun-clad woman—Israel— the fact that He had been born, persecuted and taken to Heaven, away from the possibility of destruction, is of paramount importance. Israel is looking for the Messiah. He will establish the Kingdom of God, with Jerusalem as His world capital. He will "rule all nations with a rod of iron."[24] The Apocalypse is proclaiming that the Messiah was Jesus Christ and that He will return safely from God's throne again!

Satan attempted to destroy the Man Child. At His birth, the dragon attempted to annihilate Jesus by having Herod kill all the children born in Bethlehem that were under two years of age.[25] After His baptism, the devil ventured to destroy Him with temptation. During His ministry, the serpent endeavored to have His own people of Nazareth kill Him when He ministered in the synagogue.[26] Finally, the dragon influenced the chief priests, scribes, council members and elders of Israel to demand His death.[27] The leaders of Israel carried Jesus before Pilate, who was the representative of Caesar, and satan compelled Pilate to condemn Him.[28] It was satan who incited the Jews to declare, "His blood be on us, and on our children."[29] It was satan who directed the Roman soldiers to torture Him. It was satan who guided the hammer that nailed Jesus to the cross. It was satan who, in fiendish glee, carried Jesus into death and hell.[30] Satan, however, had no legal right to hold Christ. The penalty of sin is death, but Jesus was sinless.[31] Therefore, He was raised from the dead by the power of the Father and ascended to the throne.

The Apocalypse depicts the Man Child as One who holds in His hand an iron scepter through which He is to rule all the nations.[32] This will occur during the millennial reign of Jesus, when He will rule with the Church for a thousand years.[33] Those under the rule are the unredeemed who did not bow to satan during the period of time called the tribulation, but who did not receive Jesus as Christ either. At Calvary, the serpent used the nations to crucify Christ. During the millennium, Christ will use the Church to rule the nations.

The Sun-Clad Woman in the Wilderness

John pictured that, once satan knew he could not destroy the Man Child, he would turn his wrath upon the sun-clad woman (Israel). The woman fled into the wilderness where God had provided protection for 1260 days, or three and a half years. As the birth and ascension of Christ are separated by His life, yet not shown in the Apocalypse, the ascension and the flight of the sun-clad woman are separated by 2,000 years of history. John painted the canvas from the viewpoint of eternity; thus 2,000 years is insignificant. Israel's flight into the wilderness refers to the last half week of prophetic sorrow prophesied by the prophet Daniel.[34] Daniel proclaims that one will come who will be the incarnation of satan, even as Jesus is the incarnation of the Father. He will rule for one prophetic week, or seven years, and in the middle of the week he will stop religious worship and begin a systematic persecution of Israel. This half week, (three and one-half years) or 1260 days will be called the great day of Jacob's trouble.[35] The fact that God has already counted the days of the great tribulation show the Father's concern for the suffering of the sun-clad woman. The concern of Jesus for Israel's suffering during these events is recorded in Matthew, chapter 24. Jesus warned:

So when you see standing in the holy place "the abomination that causes desolation," spoken of through the prophet Daniel—let the reader understand—then let those who are in Judea flee to the mountains. Let no one on the roof of his house go down to take anything out of the house. Let no one in the field go back to get his cloak. How dreadful it will be in those days for pregnant women and nursing mothers! Pray that your flight will not take place in winter or on the Sabbath. For then there will be great distress, unequaled from the beginning of the world until now—and never to be equaled again.[36]

The War in Heaven

The spectacle of a war in the heavens being fought between Michael the archangel with his angels, and the dragon with his demon spirits, is not called a sign in

John's explanation of the painting. Many cannot accept that satan has a place in the heavens. But the Book of Job, chapter 1, indicates that he has access to heaven. The warfare of the Church is with spiritual wickedness in the heavenlies.[37] The prophet Isaiah wrote that the day would come when the Lord would "punish the host of the high ones that are on high..."[38] The vista painted by John of a war fought in Heaven between satan and his demons and Michael and his angels, portrays that event.

John wrote, "Woe to the inhabitants of the earth and of the sea! for the devil is come down unto you, having great wrath, because he knoweth that he hath but a short time."[39] His time, according to the writings of Daniel and of the Apocalypse, lasts only seven years. This is called the "time of Jacob's trouble" because the name *Israel* (prince of God) was given as a spiritual name to Jacob (the supplanter).[40] Jacob is the name for Israel without spiritual relationship. The nation of Israel, which will have been gathered back into the land of promise, will not have returned to her spiritual relationship. Satan will see this as an opportunity to destroy her. He will persecute "the woman which brought forth the man child."[41]

At the mid-point of the time of Jacob's trouble (the tribulation), a man who is the incarnation of satan—even as Jesus was the incarnation of God—will desecrate the rebuilt temple in Jerusalem.[42] This will leave three and one-half years of great tribulation and great persecution for Israel. If the nation of Israel did not receive some protection during this period of time, the sun-clad woman would be destroyed. Thus John writes:

The woman was given the two wings of a great eagle, so that she might fly to the place prepared for her in the desert, where she would be taken care of for a time, times and half a time, out of the serpent's reach.[43]

"A time and times and half a time" is the apocalyptic way of saying three and one-half years. During this time Israel is hidden in "the wilderness." The wilderness has a peculiar reference to Israel in her national history. The prophet Ezekiel wrote that Israel was in "the wilderness of the land of Egypt."[44] Israel spent 40 years in the "wilderness" when she refused to enter the promised land. Ezekiel prophesied that God would bring the nation of Israel into the wilderness so He could plead with her face to face.[45] The prophet Hosea reveals that in the time Israel would spend "in the wilderness," they would be able to approach God.[46]

Because the dragon cannot destroy the sun-clad woman, he goes to "make war with the remnant of her seed."[47] John's portrait of the Man Child is not complete until the viewer recognizes that He is the first of many children. There is always a "remnant of her seed" necessary for the fulfillment of the covenants between God and man. God gave an eternal, unconditional covenant to Abraham saying that he would have a seed.[48] God gave a covenant concerning the land of Palestine. It is imperative that there be a "remnant" to receive the promised inheritance.[49] God gave a covenant that promises Israel's restoration as a nation.[50] The apostle Paul stated that God does not number all the physical seed of Abraham as descendants; rather, the promises are to those who are in faith.[51] Paul also wrote, concerning Israel in the last days:

And so all Israel will be saved, as it is written: "The deliverer will come from Zion; He will turn godlessness away from Jacob. And this is My covenant with them when I take away their sins."[52]

By "all Israel," Paul refers to the believing remnant of Jews at the second coming of Christ. This remnant will turn to Jesus, the Elder Brother/Man Child, during the tribulation period. The Man Child is the Christ of the Apocalypse.

End Notes

1. Gen. 37:3,5. **2.** Gen. 37:9-10. **3.** Ezek. 16:32. **4.** Rev. 12:9. **5.** Is. 14:12-15 (NIV). **6.** Ezek. 28:13-15 (NIV). **7.** Dan. 10:13; Eph. 6:12. **8.** Dan. 2:31-45. **9.** Dan. 7:8. **10.** Rev. 12:4. **11.** II Cor. 4:4; Eph. 6:10-18; Col. 2:15. **12.** Isa. 14:13. **13.** Ex. 1:22. **14.** Josh. 7. **15.** Rev. 12:15-16. **16.** Rev. 12:17. **17.** Luke 2:4. **18.** Luke 2:40. **19.** Luke 2:42-47. **20.** Matt. 2:16. **21.** John 2:9; Matt. 8:26. **22.** Matt. 4:10. **23.** I John 1:1. **24.** Rev. 12:5. **25.** Matt. 2:16. **26.** Luke 4:28-30. **27.** Mark 15:1. **28.** Mark 15:1-5,15. **29.** Matt. 27:25. **30.** Rom 10:7. **31.** Rom 6:23. **32.** Rev. 12:5. **33.** Rev. 20:6. **34.** Dan. 9:27. **35.** Rev. 11:2; 13:5; Jer. 30:7. **36.** Matt. 24:15-21 (NIV). **37.** Eph. 6:12. **38.** Isa. 24:21. **39.** Rev. 12:12. **40.** Jer. 30:7. **41.** Rev. 12:13. **42.** Dan. 9:27. **43.** Rev. 12:14 (NIV). **44.** Ezek. 20:36. **45.** Ezek. 20:35. **46.** Hos. 2:14-23. **47.** Rev. 12:17. **48.** Gen. 12:1-3; 13:14-17; 15:4-21; 17:1-8; 22:17-18. **49.** Deut. 30:1-10; Ezek. 11:16-21; 36:21-38. **50.** Ezek. 16:60. **51.** Rom. 9:6. **52.** Rom. 11:26-27 (NIV).

Portrait 6

Jesus on Mount Zion[*]

John's next painting is a familiar scene from his childhood that is viewed in a new light. Mount Zion, in the southeastern section of the city of Jerusalem, seems to be crowned with the temple as it was before its destruction by Titus of Rome. Once more the courts of Zion are filled with worshipers; the air is filled with the joyful shouts of the inhabitants. In his vision, John paints Jerusalem in all her splendor. His eyes are filled with tears both of joy and sorrow. Like the exiles carried captive into Babylon, John, still a captive in the flesh on the island of Patmos, cannot control his emotions when he remembers Zion. The brush strokes

---

*   Rev. 14:1-13.

show great passion, excitement and flair for the grandeur of the temple.

From his vision, John paints the men of Israel as assembled in the same formation that their ancestors used when they had crossed the wilderness. Tribal banners stir in the breeze that passes over Zion. Behind each of the 12 waving banners stand 12,000 men from each tribe of Israel. Together they form an army of 144,000 men. John's portrait of each man indicates that they are sexually pure, redeemed, pure of speech, and without any sin. On the forehead of each he writes the name of his God!

Their formation, however, does not center on the tabernacle, as had that of the assembly in the wilderness. Nor is the temple the center of the masterpiece. In the midst of the 144,000 John paints, again, the Lamb!

In this portrait the Lamb does not have the marks of crucifixion. Its fleece is full, clean and white. The Lamb is the center of the adoration of the 144,000 sons of Israel, and they sing a new song to Him—an aria that even John cannot learn.

The music is felt more than it is seen. It is supplied by a voice from the throne that sounds like the flowing of many rivers, the report of thunder, and the melody of a myriad of harps. Wherever the Lamb is portrayed, the 144,000 sons of Zion accompany Him, and the sounds of a heavenly orchestra radiate from the painting.

John paints three angels flying in the midst of the heavens in response to the presence of the Lamb. The first angel preaches the everlasting gospel to the earth. The second angel cries that "Babylon" has fallen and that Babylon was the city that had made all nations drink of the wine of fornication. The third angel announces that those who had worshiped the Antichrist and received the mark of his ownership would be tormented with fire and brimstone in the very presence of the Lamb—Jesus Christ!

The City of God

When John, through the Holy Spirit, sketched this portrait of the Christ of the Apocalypse, he had a Jewish viewer in mind. Can you see the walls of Jerusalem? Can you hear the noise of the merchants in the narrow streets? Can you smell the sacrifice and the frankincense emanating from the temple? Do you feel her passion for freedom and the militancy of her once enslaved peoples? Can you shout with the armies that present themselves to the long-awaited Messiah? Then perhaps you have some understanding of the painting already! The color, detail and victorious strokes of the brush appeal to anyone who ever has been enslaved and set free—even from the bondage of sin!

John's earlier vision, the one of the lamb that had been slain, was presented with the expectation that the whole world would view the canvas and see their salvation. The Lamb on Mount Zion is presented with a bias toward the sons of Israel. The Messiah reigning on Mount Zion is God's promise to His chosen people! The vision of John coincides with Isaiah's revelation of the redeemed Israel praising God on Zion.

The desert and the parched land will be glad; the wilderness will rejoice and blossom. Like the crocus, it will burst into bloom; it will rejoice greatly and shout for joy. The glory of Lebanon will be given to it, the splendor of Carmel and Sharon; they will see the glory of the Lord, the splendor of our God.

Strengthen the feeble hands, steady the knees that give way; say to those with fearful hearts, "Be strong, do not fear; your God will come, He will come with vengeance; with divine retribution He will come to save you."

Then will the eyes of the blind be opened and the ears of the deaf unstopped. Then will the lame leap like a deer, and the mute tongue shout for joy. Water will gush forth in the wilderness and streams in the desert. The burning sand will become a pool, the thirsty ground bubbling springs. In the haunts where jackals once lay, grass and reeds and papyrus will grow.

And a highway will be there; it will be called the Way of Holiness. The unclean will not journey on it; it will be for those who walk in that

Way; wicked fools will not go about on it. No lion will be there, nor will any ferocious beast get up on it; they will not be found there. But only the redeemed will walk there, and the ransomed of the Lord will return. They will enter Zion with singing; everlasting joy will crown their heads. Gladness and joy will overtake them, and sorrow and sighing will flee away.[1]

Isaiah's prophecy of the redeemed on Zion, like John's vision of the 144,000, is filled with the sounds of music and joy. Both John and Isaiah see the destruction and terror of the period of tribulation, but they also see the joy of the millennial reign of Christ. Because of the presence of the Lamb on Zion, the blind will see, the deaf hear, the dumb speak, and the lame leap for joy. Isaiah wrote:

The moon will be abashed, the sun ashamed; for the Lord Almighty will reign on Mount Zion and in Jerusalem, and before its elders, gloriously.[2]

The beauty and the glory of the Lamb is such that the moon will be embarrassed and the sun mortified when their lights are compared with His brilliance. The authority of the religious leaders of Israel will be eclipsed in the light of His command and sovereignty. The Lamb, headquartered on Mount Zion, will have more authority over Israel than Moses had when he led the exodus from Egypt. The Lamb, commanding from

Mount Zion, will have more control over the 144,000 men of God than Joshua had when he led Israel to victory after victory in the conquest of the promised land. The strength of the army on Zion is its solidarity with the Lamb. Neither in the time of tribulation nor in the millennial reign of Christ can that union be dissolved. God laughs at those who try!

> *Why do the nations conspire and the peoples plot in vain? The kings of the earth take their stand and the rulers gather together against the Lord and against His Anointed One. "Let us break their chains," they say, "and throw off their fetters." The One enthroned in heaven laughs; the Lord scoffs at them. Then He rebukes them in His anger and terrifies them in His wrath, saying, "I have installed My King on Zion, My holy hill."*[3]

John's painting of the Lamb on Mount Zion is colored with the brilliant pigment of victory. Jerusalem has been conquered by many despots. The atrocities of these villainous rulers are painted in the blackness of evil and in the crimson of blood. The sufferings of the Jews are recorded in holocaustic pictures and paintings of dark gloom and scarlet suffering. The antichrist and his army of spiritual slaves will attempt to cover Zion and the government of God with the color of evil, sin and rebellion. But God in the heavens laughs, and with one stroke the brush paints a white lamb into the scene.

There is a Lamb on Zion and because of Him, the crimson of a blood-like sunset is changed to the golden yellow of sunrise. There is a Lamb on Zion and because of Him, the dark hues of rebellion and sin are changed to the bright tints of obedience and redemption. There is a Lamb on Zion and because of Him, 12 banners of shimmering color unfurl in the breeze. Thus the sky above Zion, in the painting, is filled with bright pigment. Twelve flags waving on Mount Zion indicate that the government of God will be re-established on the earth; His capital city will be Jerusalem; and His Kingdom will have a Lamb on its throne!

The 144,000

John painted 144,000 sons of Israel, each of whom were distinct from all other men in that they had the name of the Father of the Lamb written on their foreheads. John was surely aware of the prophecies of Ezekiel, which told of the men of Jerusalem who would weep and wail over the abominable things happening within the city during the period of the tribulation. Ezekiel wrote:

Now the glory of the God of Israel went up from above the cherubim, where it had been, and moved to the threshold of the temple. Then the Lord called to the man clothed in linen who had the writing kit at his side and said to him, "Go throughout the city of Jerusalem and put a mark on the foreheads of those who grieve and lament over all the detestable things that are done in it." As I listened, He said to the others, "Follow him through the city and kill, without showing pity or compassion. Slaughter old men, young men and maidens, women and children, but do not touch anyone who has the mark. Begin at My sanctuary." So they began with the elders who were in front of the temple.[4]

The angel dressed in linen was to put a mark on the forehead of the men who were moved with pity and sorrow for Jerusalem. Was this mark the name of their God? If so, the vision seen by Ezekiel and the mural of the Apocalypse present the same episode. John saw the tribulation judgment held until the men were sealed "in their foreheads."[5] Ezekiel saw that it was a mark on the forehead that saved the servants of God from God's great judgment. The 144,000 are sons of God who are marked with the name of their God.

An angel of God with the *sphragis* (the stamp-seal) of God seals 12,000 from each tribe of the children of Israel, but he does not seal them in the order of their birth.[6] Reuben and his tribe are the firstborn of Jacob.[7] Judah is the fourth of Jacob's children, but John notes that his tribe is the first to be sealed by the angel. Reuben is to be sealed only after Judah has received the seal of protection. Jacob said of Reuben:

Reuben, thou are my firstborn, my might, and the beginning of my strength, the excellency of dignity, and the excellency of power: unstable as water, thou shalt not excel; because thou wentest up to thy father's bed; then defiledst thou it: he went up to my couch.[8]

The number two is the biblical number for man. God is a one and the Godhead is a three, but man was made a little less than God. God said, "Let Us make man in Our image" and He "created He him; male and female created He them."[9] Because man sinned, he became "unstable." Man became a two looking for the one who would give him stability. From the tribe of Judah came the One for whom man was seeking—Jesus Christ!

The tribe of Gad is the third tribe to be sealed by the angel, and the eighth son of Jacob. Jacob's blessing of Gad was that he would be an "overcomer."[10] The "overcomer" is number three in John's vision of the sealing of the tribes. The source of the overcomer is the divine Trinity—the Father, Son and Holy Spirit.

The fourth tribe to be sealed with the name of the Father on the forehead is the tribe of Asher. Four is the number for the earth and Asher was promised, "Out of Asher his bread shall be fat."[11] To be fat is to be fleshly or earthly.

The tribe of Naphtali is sealed next. Naphtali is blessed to give "goodly words."[12] Man can receive information through the five senses. He who receives the "goodly words" is the fifth to be anointed by the angel.

Manasseh is sixth in John's vision. The tribe of Manasseh replaces the tribe of Dan. The tribe of Dan does not receive the anointing name of the Father. Jacob said of Dan:

Dan shall judge his people, as one of the tribes of Israel. Dan shall be a serpent by the way, an adder in the path, that biteth the horse heels, so that his rider shall fall backward.[13]

From Dan would come one who would be an accuser of God's people. From the tribe of Dan one would come who would be like a serpent. The power of the serpent cannot touch those marked by the angel; therefore, Dan is excluded from the imprint of the inkhorn.

John lists the tribe of Simeon after Manasseh. Jacob said of Simeon and his brother Levi:

Simeon and Levi are brothers—their swords are weapons of violence. Let me not enter their council, let me not join their assembly, for they have killed men in their anger and hamstrung oxen as they pleased. Cursed be their anger, so fierce, and their fury, so cruel! I will scatter them in Jacob and disperse them in Israel.[14]

The tribes of Simeon and Levi are used to portray the judgmental nature of the tribulation. John lists them as the seventh and eighth tribes. The judgment will be complete (seven) and a new beginning will quickly follow, for eight is the number of new things.

Issachar is the ninth tribe listed by John. Issachar is called "a servant unto tribute" by Jacob.[15] It is interesting to note that there are exactly nine gifts of the Spirit which serve the Church and give her commendation. During the millennial reign of Jesus Christ, the gifts of the Spirit will pass away for the Church will not need them.[16] The Church herself will become a "servant of tribute" to Jesus.

The tenth tribe as listed by John, Zebulun, whom Jacob calls a "haven of ships," is also the tenth son of Jacob.[17] The name *Zebulun* means "bestow honor or dwell with." Ten is the number of multiplication. Jesus will bestow honor and dwell with His Church for a thousand years.

The tribe of Joseph is the eleventh one sealed, according to John. Joseph was blessed by Jacob, who said of him:

Joseph is a fruitful vine, a fruitful vine near a spring, whose branches climb over a wall. With bitterness archers attacked him; they shot at him with hostility. But his bow remained steady, his strong arms stayed limber, because of the hand of the Mighty One of Jacob, because of the Shepherd, the Rock of Israel, because of your father's God, who helps you, because of the Almighty, who blesses you with blessings of the heavens above, blessings of the deep that lies below, blessings of the breast and womb.

Your father's blessings are greater than the blessings of the ancient mountains, than the bounty of the age-old hills. Let all these rest on the head of Joseph, on the brow of the prince among his brothers.[18]

Eleven is a combination of four, the earth, and seven, the perfect. God will make a new heaven and a new earth.[19] The "overcomers" will occupy the new heaven and new earth as pillars in His temple. They will live in the new Jerusalem and they will have His new name.[20] These "overcomers" are those delivered from the "hour of temptation, which shall come upon all the world" (the raptured Church) as well as the 144,000 Jewish witnesses and all those of Israel who overcame because of the word of their testimony. Their "blessings" will be greater than all the other blessings God has given to men.

The tribe of Benjamin is the twelfth in both John's vision and in Jacob's blessing. In his early days he shall *taraph,* pluck off or pull to pieces, and in his latter days he shall divide the spoil.[21] Benjamin, whose name means "son of my right hand," represents the Son who has plucked off evil and pulled to pieces the power of sin, and who will sit on "the right hand of the Majesty on high."[22] It is Jesus, the Lamb, who will divide the spoil. Jesus is the new Benjamin who will be the judicial authority of the Kingdom of God. Twelve thousand men, representing judicial authority multiplied to the power of infinity, will be formed into 12 tribes, which depicts social authority expounded to its ultimate. They will focus upon a throne, the apex of authority in Heaven and earth, which will be on Mount Zion.[23] There they will worship the Lamb!

A Voice From Heaven

John describes a musical fugue in which the subject is announced by a voice from Heaven that sounds like the pounding of surf or the roaring of a waterfall accompanied by a multitude of harps. The chorus of the fugue is sung by a choir made up of the 144,000 sons of Israel on Mount Zion. Could any musical genius imagine such an extravaganza? The lead solo's voice is God's. He is accompanied in Heaven by a multitude of harpists playing in unison. Once the refrain of the harps is fully received, a male chorus of 144,000 joyful voices rock the hills of earth with their refrain from Zion. With great feeling for the occasion, the prophet Zephaniah proclaimed:

Sing, O Daughter of Zion; shout aloud, O Israel! Be glad and rejoice with all your heart, O Daughter of Jerusalem! The Lord has taken away your punishment, He has turned back your enemy. The Lord, the King of Israel, is with you; never again will you fear any harm. On that day they will say to Jerusalem, "Do not fear, O Zion; do not let your hands hang limp. The Lord your God is with you, He is mighty to save. He will take great delight in you, He will *quiet you with His love, **He will rejoice over you with singing.*** *The sorrows for the appointed feasts I will remove from you; they are a burden and a reproach to you. At that time I will deal with all who oppressed you; I will rescue the lame and gather those who have been scattered. I will give them praise and honor in every land where they were put to shame. At that time I will gather you; at that time I will bring you home. I will give you honor and praise among all the peoples of the earth when I restore your fortunes before your very eyes,"* *says the Lord.*[24]

In John's vision, the singing of our Lord God comes from the heavens above Zion. Although Zion is to become the center of government for the world, Heaven will still be the center of authority for the cosmos. The voice of God is compared to a Niagara Falls and to the rumble of thunder because it is the sound of unmeasurable power. The voice of infinite might is heard against the lovely, lilting, soft, melodious strings of harps. God's voice comes in sweet, unmeasurable power. John received a demonstration of this fact when he was told to eat the book of the Word of God.

And I went unto the angel, and said unto him, Give me the little book. And he said unto me, Take it, and eat it up; and it shall make thy belly bitter, but it shall be in thy mouth sweet as honey.[25]

Unmeasurable power is frightening and can be a little bitter to the human soul, but God sweetens His authority with gentleness and love—the sound of the harp.

A New Song

And they sang a new song before the throne and before the four living creatures and the elders. No one could learn the song except the 144,000 who had been redeemed from the earth.[26]

Christianity is a singing faith. Most religious persuasions do not use song as an expression of worship. Some use chants or sacred words, but the born again Christian has a joy in his heart that can be expressed only in song. The angels do not sing. They did not sing at the birth of Christ.[27] ("And the angel *said* unto them, Fear not: for, behold, I bring you good tidings of great joy, which shall be to all people" [Luke 2:10].) Disciples of Christ sing because they alone of all of God's creation know what it was to be in sin and death and to have been delivered. Deliverance always produces a song!

The redeemed Jews, having been delivered (as were Moses and the children of Israel) from the great tribulation, have a song.

...and sang the song of Moses the servant of God and the song of the Lamb: Great and marvelous are Your deeds, Lord God Almighty. Just and true are Your ways, King of the ages.[28]

The song of Moses is found in Exodus 15:

Then Moses and the Israelites sang this song to the Lord: "I will sing to the Lord, for He is highly exalted. The horse and its rider He has hurled into the sea. The Lord is my strength and my song; He has become my salvation. He is my God, and I will praise Him, my father's God, and I will exalt Him. The Lord is a warrior; the Lord is His name. Pharaoh's chariots and his army He has hurled into the sea. The best of Pharaoh's officers are drowned in the Red Sea. The deep waters have covered them; they sang to the depths like a stone.

"Your right hand, O Lord, was majestic in power. Your right hand, O Lord, shattered the enemy. In the greatness of Your majesty You threw down those who opposed You. You unleashed Your burning anger; it consumed them like stubble. By the blast of Your nostrils the waters piled up. The surging waters stood firm like a wall; the deep waters congealed in the heart of the sea.

"The enemy boasted, 'I will pursue, I will overtake them. I will divide the spoils; I will gorge myself on them. I will draw my sword and my hand will destroy them.' But You blew with Your breath, and the sea covered them. They sank like lead in the mighty waters.

"Who among the gods is like You, O Lord? Who is like You—majestic in holiness, awesome in glory, working wonders? You stretched out Your right hand and the earth swallowed them.

"In Your unfailing love You will lead the people You have redeemed. In Your strength You will guide them to Your holy dwelling. The nations will hear and tremble; anguish will grip the people of Philistia. The chiefs of Edom will be terrified, the leaders of Moab will be seized with trembling, the people of Canaan will melt away; terror and dread will fall upon them. By the power of Your arm they will be as still as a stone—until Your people pass by, O Lord, until the people You bought pass by. You will bring them in and plant them on the mountain of Your inheritance—the place, O Lord, You made for Your dwelling, the sanctuary, O Lord, Your hands established. The Lord will reign for ever and ever."[29]

The redeemed house of Israel will remember the deliverance of the nation from the hand of Pharaoh and compare it to their deliverance from the hand of the antichrist. They also will sing the song of the Lamb, Jesus Christ! Could that song include: "the Lamb has thrown the devil, the antichrist and the false prophet into the lake of fire and brimstone"?[30] The similarity is striking!

Moral Purity

The 144,000 sons of Israel are morally pure.

These are those who did not defile themselves with women, for they kept themselves pure. They follow the Lamb wherever He goes. They were purchased from among men and offered as firstfruits to God and the Lamb. No lie was found in their mouths; they are blameless.[31]

Those who will be with the Lamb must be morally pure. Of all the sins that man can commit, the Holy Spirit points out that the 144,000 men on Zion are considered "blameless" because they are sexually pure and have not perverted the truth. To not be defiled with women does not mean that all of the 144,000 men were single. Marriage is an honorable estate and is undefiled in the sight of God.[32] The 144,000 sons of God have not been either fornicators or adulterers sexually. Neither have they been desecrated by spiritual adultery, which is the spiritual sin of idolatry.[33] Idolatry is breaking a covenant with God by having relationship with supposed gods who are, in reality, demons. According to the prophet Jeremiah, God divorced the nation of Israel because she had committed adultery with idols.

I gave faithless Israel her certificate of divorce and sent her away because of all her adulteries. Yet I saw that her unfaithful sister Judah had no fear; she also went out and committed adultery. Because Israel's immorality mattered so little to her, she defiled the land and committed adultery with stone and wood.[34]

Sexual sin is a physical manifestation of spiritual idolatry. It was considered a form of idolatry by the Jerusalem counsel. Thus the gentile converts to Christianity were forbidden, in the only laws given them, to practice either idolatry or sexual immorality.[35]

Satan is the father of liars. Jesus said:

You belong to your father, the devil, and you want to carry out your father's desire. He was a murderer from the beginning, not holding to the truth, for there is no truth in him. When he lies, he speaks his native language, for he is a liar and the father of lies.[36]

The 144,000 sons of God will have nothing to do with satan. They will not worship him through idolatry. They will not speak his word through lies. They are not like their ancestors, the prophets, of whom Jeremiah wrote:

And among the prophets of Jerusalem I have seen something horrible: They commit adultery and live a lie. They strengthen the hands of evil-doers, so that no one turns from his wicked-ness. They are all like Sodom to Me; the people of Jerusalem are like Gomorrah.[37]

A man who worships God through Jesus Christ, without any form of self-interest, and who speaks nothing but the truth (Jesus is the truth) is morally clean.[38] One hundred and forty-four thousand such men will stand with the Lamb on Mount Zion. They will be the first of many who will find a relationship with Jesus during the tribulation period.

The Firstfruits

John calls the 144,000 sons of Israel the "first-fruits." The concept of firstfruits comes from the Jewish feast of Pentecost. This was the celebration of the harvest. The first part of the harvest was brought to the temple to celebrate God's grace and blessing on the rest of the harvest. These 144,000, then, are the evidence of a greater harvest of the children of Israel who are to come to the Lamb through the tribulation. So as the events of Pentecost foretold the beginning of the Church Age, the 144,000 before the Lamb foretell the redemption of Israel.

The firstfruits offering was the most precious contribution God received from Israel. The Day of Atonement was for the benefit of the cleansing of the people. The oblation of Pentecost was the offering that was brought to the temple and dedicated exclusively to God, without hope of benefit by the people. The Jewish feast of Pentecost was a time of rejoicing and a time of renewal of faith. For the Church, the Day of Pentecost alone produced 3,000 new converts.[39] The presentation of the 144,000 "firstfruits" to the Lamb will produce a messenger of hope, one who carries the everlasting gospel to "every nation, and kindred, and tongue, and people."[40] It also will induce a message of judgment on the world system.[41] To those who take of the Lamb, the messenger brings an announcement of hope and life. To those who reject the Lamb, the messenger carries a declaration of affliction, death and judgment. Paul wrote of those who experienced the power of the first Pentecost:

> *To the one we are the savour of death unto death; and to the other the savour of life unto life.*[42]

The painting of the Lamb and the 144,000 sons of Israel is one portrait. The canvas cannot be seen without viewing both. He, Jesus, is a "firstfruit."

> *But Christ has indeed been raised from the dead, the firstfruits of those who have fallen asleep.*[43]

In John's portrait of the Lamb of God surrounded by the 144,000 sons of Israel, both the Lamb and the 144,000 are "firstfruits." The Lamb stands on the temple ground to represent the Atonement and the 144,000 stand with Him to depict Pentecost. Because of the Atonement, with its forgiveness of sin, and because of Pentecost, with its power in the spirit, banners of victory wave in Zion.

End Notes

1. Is. 35:1-10 (NIV). **2.** Isa. 24:23 (NIV). **3.** Ps. 2:1-6 (NIV. **4.** Ezek. 9:3-6 (NIV). **5.** Rev. 7:3. **6.** Rev. 7:5-8. **7.** Gen. 49. **8.** Gen. 49:3-4. **9.** Gen. 1:26,27. **10.** Gen. 49:19. **11.** Gen. 49:20. **12.** Gen. 49:21. **13.** Gen. 49:16-17. **14.** Gen. 49:5-7 (NIV). **15.** Gen. 49:15. **16.** I Cor. 13:10. **17.** Gen. 49:13. **18.** Gen. 49:22-26 (NIV). **19.** Rev. 21:1. **20.** Rev. 3:21. **21.** Gen. 49:27. **22.** Heb. 1:3. **23.** Rev. 7:15; 14:3. **24.** Zeph. 3:14-20 (NIV). **25.** Rev. 10:9. **26.** Rev. 14:3 (NIV). **27.** Luke 2:8-14. **28.** Rev. 15:3 (NIV). **29.** Ex. 15:1-18 (NIV) **30.** Rev. 20:10. **31.** Rev. 14:4-5 (NIV). **32.** Heb. 13:4. **33.** Col. 3:5. **34.** Jer. 3:8-9 (NIV). **35.** Acts 15:29. **36.** John 8:44 (NIV). **37.** Jer. 23:14 (NIV). **38.** John 14:6. **39.** Acts 2:41. **40.** Rev. 14:6. **41.** Rev. 14:8. **42.** II Cor. 2:16a. **43.** I Cor. 15:20 (NIV).

Portrait 7
The Son of Man[*]

In this portrait gallery of the Christ of the Apocalypse, we have seen Jesus in many forms. A colossus. A gem of great brilliance. A mighty angel. A slaughtered lamb. A lamb without spot or blemish.

Each apparition, painted as he saw it, stirred feelings of wonder and awe in the artist. The next vision brought mixed sensations. He felt its intensity. He was filled with nostalgia. A long-forgotten yearning was revived. John was touched with memories of love. This new piece for his art collection brought fulfillment as no other portrait had.

John saw his friend. His teacher. His Lord. In His flesh, Jesus had been carried into Heaven on a cloud.[1]

---

*   Rev. 14:14-20.

Here John once again paints his beloved Jesus. He paints Jesus sitting on a cloud. The Man on the cloud has the same familiar form that walked the dusty roads of Palestine. The way Jesus sits on the cloud reminds John of their time together at His last Passover. Jesus is wearing the same white seamless robe. It is decorated with the same blue rabbinic tassels Jesus wore in His earthly ministry.

Jesus had never looked at John with eyes like fearsome laser beams. No! Jesus' eyes were not the eyes of the colossus. The eyes of Jesus were soft. Filled with love. Eyes that blessed. The Man on the cloud had the familiar eyes of love that had blessed John for so many years, so many times.

Two things about the Christ on the cloud were not familiar. Jesus had used a walking stick in the wilderness. The tools from the carpentry shop also were natural to Him. John had seen Jesus use them many times. Sometimes Jesus had carried a shepherd's staff. But this Jesus of the cloud held a sharp sickle in His hand!

Second, Jesus had worn a prayer cloth in public. Alone with the disciples, He had allowed His long shimmering tassels to blow freely in the winds of the Galilee. But this Jesus of the cloud was crowned with a diadem of pure gold!

Portrayed with Jesus are the two angels John had seen at the ascension of his Lord.[2] At that time the angels said to the disciples:

"Men of Galilee," they said, "why do you stand here looking into the sky? This same Jesus, who has been taken from you into heaven, will come back in the same way you have seen Him go into heaven."[3]

John paints one of the angels as coming out of the temple. The angel cries with a voice so loud that he is heard by the Son of Man, who is sitting upon the cloud. He announces to the Christ that it is time to reap. The harvest of the earth is ready!

In the revelation, John paints Jesus as plunging the sharp sickle into the earth and gathering the harvest into bales. The Lord of the harvest then separates the good grain from the weeds and tares.

Another angel is portrayed as coming out of the temple with a sickle. This angel is told, by a fourth angel who comes out of the altar, to thrust in his sickle and gather the clusters of the grape vine. The grapes that are reaped are cast into an enormous winepress. The grapes are crushed. The grapes produce human blood—a river of blood five feet deep!

The Man Who Rides a Cloud

After His post-resurrection appearances to the apostles, Jesus ascended into the heavens on a cloud.[4] He promised that He would return to earth on the clouds.[5] The clouds symbolized the presence of God to the nation of Israel. In their deliverance from bondage in Egypt, God directed the exodus through a pillar of a cloud by day and a pillar of fire by night.[6] God came to Moses on mount Sinai in a "thick cloud."[7] The presence of God in the tabernacle was denoted by a cloud covering the tent.[8] When the sacrifices of Israel were accepted, a cloud covered the mercy seat of the ark of the covenant.[9] When God's presence filled the temple, the priests were not able to minister because of the glory of the cloud.[10] The prophet Isaiah wrote that the Lord of Israel rode on a "swift cloud."[11] When Jesus was translated before the apostles, "a bright cloud" overshadowed them.[12]

The One who rides the cloud is called "the Son of Man." The New Testament notes 80 times that Jesus is called by the title, "Son of Man." The title denotes God's authority on earth to forgive sins, authority over the Sabbath, authority over the harvest, and authority over the demonic kingdom.[13]

Jesus asked the question of the disciples, "Who do people say that the Son of Man is?" John's vision of the Son of Man riding on a cloud is the answer to that question. Jesus, as Son of Man, is incarnate deity! The One who led the children of Israel in the exodus as a cloud by day and a pillar of fire at night was Jesus! The presence that filled the tabernacle with glory was Jesus! The God of the cloud of Sinai was Jesus! Jesus who ascended into Heaven on a cloud was God and the Son of Man who returns to earth riding on a cloud is God! The gold crown He wears is the victor's crown! The victory is already the Lord's, but He comes on a cloud to receive the spoil. The booty is a harvest of grain that represents the sons of the Kingdom who heard and responded to the Word.[15] Others will harvest the booty of the vine of the earth and prepare it for the winepress of wrath. He who rides on the cloud wears a crown of gold. The produce of the Word is His. He is the victorious Lord of the harvest!

The Voice From the Temple

Before Moses made the tabernacle in the wilderness, before David planned the temple, and before Solomon had the temple built in Jerusalem, God had a temple in Heaven. Moses was told to build and furnish the tabernacle according to the pattern.[16] The word translated "pattern" comes from the Hebrew *tabniyth,* and can be translated as "structure." John heard the Christ of the Apocalypse state that overcomers would become a "pillar in the temple of My God."[17] Those who come through the "great tribulation" will serve God before the throne in His temple.[18] John painted the original ark of the testament in the temple of God that was located in Heaven.[19]

John's brush reveals another angel in the painting, one crying to the Son of Man from out of the temple. "It is time to reap the harvest of the earth!" If the Son of Man is the Lord Jesus Christ, how could a mere angel give Him instruction? The angel does not cry out to instruct, but to inform! Jesus Himself said of the end times, "But of that day and hour knoweth no man, no, not the angels of heaven, but My Father only."[20] Since the angel cries from out of the temple, it is understood that he is carrying a message from the Father. The message is, "The time is come for Thee to reap; for the harvest of the earth is ripe."[21] The verb form "is ripe," *exeranthe,* means "to become dry or withered." This is a harvest that is past its time. Even as the apostle Paul was a man out of time, this is a harvest past its season.[22] There is to be another gathering after this harvest is collected, but this reaping by the Son of Man is yielded after its natural season.[23]

The harvest in season is the rapture of the Church. Paul wrote:

> *According to the Lord's own word, we tell you that we who are still alive, who are left till the coming of the Lord, will certainly not precede those who have fallen asleep. For the Lord Himself will come down from heaven, with a loud command, with the voice of the archangel and with the trumpet call of God, and the dead in Christ will rise first. After that, we who are still alive and are left will be caught up together with them in the clouds to meet the Lord in the air. And so we will be with the Lord forever.*[24]

When in God's economy will this event described by Paul occur? If there is no definite evidence in the Apocalypse as to the sequence, it still needs to be understood that the Church must be in existence at the time of the catching up. The church at Philadelphia is promised:

> *Since you have kept My command to endure patiently, I will also keep you from the hour of*

trial that is going to come upon the whole world to test those who live on the earth.[25]

That event had already occurred when the Son of Man is informed that the time for the *exeranthe* harvest has come. The withered harvest is that of the tribulation saints. It is the ingathering of those who refuse to worship the antichrist. It is the reward for those who, in spite of the fact that the Church is gone, turn in obedience to the Lord of the Church. The voice that cries out of the temple is still a voice of mercy.

The Voice From the Altar

The Son of Man is not the only one with a sharp sickle in the portrait. John writes, "And another angel came out of the temple which is in heaven, he also having a sharp sickle."[26]

The voice of the angel crying from the temple is not the only voice. A second angel comes into the portrait. This one comes from the brazen altar and he has authority to minister over the fire of the altar. This angel also cries in a loud voice, but instead of directing the Son of Man, he commands the angel with the sharp sickle;

Take your sharp sickle and gather the clusters of grapes from the earth's vine because its grapes are ripe.[27]

This is not the yield of the good grain being separated from the weeds.[28] There is no separation indicated. This is the complete judgment on the fruit of unrighteousness in the earth! The angel who directs the judgment to take pace stands at the altar because the world rejected the sacrifice of the Lamb; now they themselves become the sacrifice. The grapes are—fully ripe" because iniquity has run its full course. The result of man's sin is not fully realized until the end. Man is not only judged for what he did, or failed to do, but also for what results his sins produced through time. The Greek word John used to describe the harvest, *amazo*, is a description of grapes that are bursting with juice. Sin has matured until it is ready to run over!

The Winepress of the Wrath of God

Jesus was crucified outside the gates of the city of Jerusalem. God deems it to be proper retribution to begin His judgment at the same place. The painting takes on a gruesome aspect as John reports:

They were trampled in the winepress outside the city, and blood flowed out of the press, rising as high as the horses' bridles for a distance of 1,600 stadia.[29]

This is no light, airy painting. Gone are the sparkling jewel-like colors and golden glows of earlier scenes. This is an etching depicting pain and anguish. The grape clusters represent groupings of people. They are being squeezed by the pressure and horror of seven years of tribulation.[30] The press consists of war, famine and pestilence.[31] All of the agony, torment, affliction, torture and suffering that sin has loosed on mankind is reflected in their faces as the winepress tightens, crushing the life out of their bodies and out of their very souls. Human blood oozes from the cracks of the press, spills over the top, splatters the walls of the city and flows into a river whose current carries it five feet deep for two hundred miles, thus covering the land mass of the nation of Israel.

This same picture is drawn by the prophet Isaiah, who wrote of the Messiah:

I have trodden the winepress alone; from the nations no one was with Me. I trampled them in My anger and trod them down in My wrath; their blood spattered My garments, and I stained all My clothing. For the day of vengeance was in My heart, and the year of My redemption has come.[32]

This painting depicts a vast destruction of human life through the judgment of God within a specified area. During the tribulation period, the wickedness of the earth will be concentrated in Palestine through the antichrist. The judgment, however, will encompass the whole earth for it is the "vine of the earth" that is to be reaped. Israel of old was the vine brought out of Egypt.[33] It was a vine that produced only wild grapes.[34] The strange vine of rebellion and idolatry has reproduced itself over the whole earth; therefore, the reaping is worldwide. The root of the vine is Jerusalem, so it is outside the walls of that city that the judgment will be the most severe. It is not only the grapes that must be destroyed, but also the vine itself!

End Notes

1. Acts 1:9. **2.** Acts 1:10. **3.** Acts 1:11 (NIV). **4.** Acts 1:9. **5.** Matt. 24:30; 26:64. **6.** Ex. 13:21. **7.** Ex. 19:9. **8.** Ex. 40:34. **9.** Lev. 16:2. **10.** I Kings 8:10. **11.** Isa. 19:1. **12.** Matt. 17:5. **13.** Mark 2:10; Mark 2:28; Matt. 13:37; Matt. 13:41. **14.** Matt. 16:13. **15.** Matt. 13:38. **16.** Ex. 25:9,40. **17.** Rev. 3:12. **18.** Rev. 7:14-15. **19.** Rev. 11:19. **20.** Matt. 24:36. **21.** Rev. 14:15. **22.** I Cor. 15:8. **23.** Rev. 14:18. **24.** I Thess. 4:15-17 (NIV). **25.** Rev. 3:10 (NIV). **26.** Rev. 14:17. **27.** Rev. 14:18 (NIV). **28.** Matt. 13:38 (NIV). **29.** Rev. 14:20. **30.** Dan. 9:27. **31.** Rev. 6:1-8. **32.** Is. 63:3-4 (NIV). **33.** Ps. 80:8. **34.** Isa. 5:2-4.

Portrait 8

The One Who Comes Secretly*

From the depth of his spirit, John filled the next canvas with dark, foreboding shades that give the viewer ominous feelings of dread. The only bright spots in the painting are seven shining messengers orbiting against a blackened, sinister sky. Each messenger has a glowing bowl attached to him, and from the bowl are sent waves of destroying power upon a shadowy earth.

Did you shudder a moment as you viewed the painting? It is good that you did! Only a person who does not seriously consider the art could walk nonchalantly by

---

*   Rev. 16:1-21.

this masterpiece. If the artist has truth in him, the painting depicts horror beyond a normal man's imagination.

The painting depicts a dark green, unsavory mass of disease, infirmity and sickness being released from the bowl of one of the messengers. From the bowl of another messenger, waves of clear liquid fall until it reaches the dark blue of the ocean, where it becomes grimy red, looking like coagulated blood. From another angel's bowl, unlit fire falls upon a throne of foul blackness. Hideous creatures are painted as surrounding the throne of horror, and they cry out obscenities and blasphemies as they are burned by the dark fire, but are not consumed.

From another messenger's bowl is poured out a loathsome mixture. Where the brew touches the earth, John paints unclean demons, looking like repulsive scaly creatures, existing in the shadowy basin of the Euphrates River. The last messenger of the painting also has a bowl. From its bowl comes a dreadful beam that produces thunderbolts and hundred-pound hailstones, painted against a sky of black vapor. Where the discharge of its power falls to the ground, fearful, unlighted, fiery red chasms are seen in the earth's surface.

Etched between the unilluminated lightning and the fissures of scorching earthquakes are the faces of men. The expressions on their faces are those of terror and horror. Inscribed in the representative faces is painted the trial of those ensnared in the holocaust of judgment.

The most fearful section of the mural, however, is a sinister area that has a shape within it—which is without substance. A shadowy figure is in the painting, and yet it is not there. John does not paint a form the viewer can see, but a presence the viewer can feel. The artist takes great pains to hide the fact that, in the midst of the murky texture of the painting, a figure is hidden in the darkest portion of all. The unseen realm of angels and demons are divulged in the painting. Yet within this oppressive portion of this sinister, shadowy mural, the artist has hidden someone, as a burglar hides in a pitch-black room.

From the obscure, unilluminated darkness, a voice is heard saying, "Behold, I come as a thief. Blessed is he that watcheth, and keepeth his garments, lest he walk naked, and they see his shame."[1] Much to the viewer's surprise, the voice from the shadows is the voice of Jesus. Enclosed in dark folds of the mural is the hidden portrait of the One who comes secretly.

The Seven Messengers of Wrath

The canvas depicts seven angels who are released from the temple in Heaven to carry seven plagues to the earth.[2] The Greek word for "angel" can be translated as "messenger, a pastor, or an angel/messenger." Cherubim have wings, angels can come unrecognized as such, and pastors are human messengers.[3] All of these can be angels. John painted seven of these angels in the heavens above the earth during the last days of the tribulation period. Each angel had a broad, shallow cup. But was the cup or bowl in the angel's hand under his wing, or attached to him? Was the angel a spiritual being or a physical object? John does not say. The only word John could use to describe what he painted was "angel." Could John's messengers be a series of satellites relaying commands from the contending armies gathered from Armageddon?[4] Could the first messenger be releasing missiles filled with biological weapons against Israel? Could the angels that quickly react after the first message be commanding missiles equipped with multiple nuclear warheads that, upon discharge, corrupt the waters, darken the sun, scorch men with great heat, dry up the Euphrates River, and release the demonic powers that are already on earth? Or, since John is using apocalyptic pictures, is he simply describing the ultimate destruction of evil by seven (complete) messengers from God?

Ezekiel 38 indicates in non-apocalyptic language that the tribulation begins with a seven-year war against Israel, involving Iran, Iraq, Ethiopia, Libya, Germany, Turkey and the nations of Russia, which are drawn in reluctantly. At the end of the seven-year war, all the armies gather for a final battle at Armageddon.[5] The messages of the seven angels just precede, and are during, this battle. So is it possible that the seven messengers of John are satellites that call forth the release of missiles to the final nuclear holocaust? Whether they really are spiritual angels, or whether they turn out to be spy satellites, the message is still indisputable. These seven messengers are the harbingers of the day of wrath. They are "signs" in heaven.[6] The Greek word translated "sign" can mean a natural token or a spiritual wonder. As signs, they are meant to be conspicuous. Their presence, glowing against the dark clouds of war over the landscape of Jerusalem, designates that the "Day of the Lord" has materialized.[7]

The Day of the Lord

The Day of the Lord is a time of judgment. It is God's rejoinder to the nations for their treatment of Israel. Obadiah wrote concerning the nations:

The day of the Lord is near for all nations. As you have done, it will be done to you; your deeds will return upon your own head.[8]

Joel wrote of the "Day of the Lord":

Alas for that day! For the day of the Lord is near; it will come like destruction from the Almighty. ...Blow the trumpet in Zion; sound the alarm on My holy hill. Let all who live in the land tremble, for the day of the Lord is coming. It is close at hand—a day of darkness and gloom, a day of clouds and blackness. Like dawn spreading across the mountains a large and mighty army comes, such as never was of old nor ever will be in ages to come. ...Before them the earth shakes, the sky trembles, the sun and moon are darkened, and the stars no longer shine. The Lord thunders at the head of His army; His forces are beyond number, and mighty are those who obey His command. The day of the Lord is great; it is dreadful. Who can endure it? ...I will show wonders in the heavens and on the earth, blood and fire and billows of smoke. The sun will be turned to darkness and the moon to blood before the coming of the great and dreadful day of the Lord.[9]

Was Joel seeing the use of biological and nuclear weapons in modern warfare? They would certainly make the sun appear dark and the moon as if it were filled with blood!

Isaiah wrote of the Day of the Lord:

Wail, for the day of the Lord is near; it will come like destruction from the Almighty. Because of this, all hands will go limp, every man's heart will melt. Terror will seize them, pain and anguish will grip them; they will writhe like a woman in labor. They will look aghast at each other, their faces aflame. See, the day of the Lord is coming—a cruel day, with wrath and fierce anger—to make the land desolate and destroy the sinners within it. The stars of heaven and their constellations will not show their light. The rising sun will be darkened and the moon will not give its light. I will punish the world for its evil, the wicked for their sins. I will put an end to the arrogance of the haughty and will humble the pride of the ruthless. I will make man scarcer than pure gold, more rare than the gold of Ophir. Therefore I will make the heavens tremble; and the earth will shake from its place at the wrath of the Lord Almighty, in the day of His burning anger.[10]

The Day of the Lord will have such destructive power released in it that the constellations will not be seen from earth, the sun and moon will be as if they were darkened, and the earth will be shaken from its orbit.

The prophet Zephaniah spoke of the Day of the Lord in cataclysmic terms:

The great day of the Lord is near—near and coming quickly. Listen! The cry on the day of the Lord will be bitter, the shouting of the warrior there. That day will be a day of wrath, a day of distress and anguish, a day of trouble and ruin, a day of darkness and gloom, a day of clouds and blackness, a day of trumpet and battle cry against the fortified cities and against the corner towers. I will bring distress on the people and they will walk like blind men, because they have sinned against the Lord. Their blood will be poured out like dust and their entrails like filth. Neither their silver nor their gold will be able to save them on the day of the Lord's wrath. In the fire of His jealousy the whole world will be consumed, for He will make a sudden end of all who live in the earth. Gather together, gather together, O shameful nation, before the appointed time arrives and that day sweeps on like chaff, before the fierce anger of the Lord comes upon you, before the day of the Lord's wrath comes upon you. Seek the Lord, all you humble of the land, you who do what He commands. Seek righteousness, seek humility; perhaps you will be sheltered on the day of the Lord's anger.[11]

The apostle Peter, preaching on the Jewish feast of Pentecost, reflected on the Day of the Lord. Peter said:

I will show wonders in the heaven above and signs on the earth below, blood and fire and billows of smoke. The sun will be turned to darkness and the moon to blood before the coming of the great and glorious day of the Lord.[12]

He also wrote in his second letter:

The Lord is not slow in keeping His promise, as some understand slowness. He is patient with you, not wanting anyone to perish, but everyone to come to repentance. But the day of the Lord will come like a thief. The heavens will disappear with a roar; the elements will be destroyed by fire, and the earth and everything in it will be laid bare.[13]

"The elements will be destroyed by fire." Could there be any clearer description of a nuclear holocaust? Joel puts the Day of the Lord in its context. He writes:

Multitudes, multitudes in the valley of decision! For the day of the Lord is near in the valley of decision.[14]

The key is "the valley of decision." This is the valley of Jezreel in the plain of Esdraelon—the site of the battle of Armageddon. John's dark, dreadful painting is a vista of the cataclysmic result of the sinfulness of man.

The Thief in the Night

Peter, announcing the Day of the Lord, states that it will come "as a thief in the night."[15] Paul writes, "For you know very well that the day of the Lord will come like a thief in the night."[16] In the dark, shadowy, nondescript portion of John's mural of the Day of the Lord, the voice of Jesus is heard, "Behold, I come as a thief."[17] Why the hidden, secret Christ? Everything Jesus did, He did openly. He said:

"I have spoken openly to the world," Jesus replied. "I always taught in synagogues or at the temple, where all the Jews come together. I said nothing in secret."[18]

Yet He comes as a hidden, clandestine, evasive thief in the night in this painting!

The Time of His Coming

The timing of the final judgment and coming of Jesus Christ has always been God's secret. Men have written books predicting the coming of Jesus and the rapture of the Church, only to have their predictions proven false. God alone knows the moment of the events.[19]

Paul thought that the rapture would occur during his lifetime. He wrote:

Then we which are alive and remain shall be caught up together with them in the clouds to meet the Lord in the air: and so shall we ever be with the Lord.[20]

The apostle fully expected to be alive when the rapture transpired. No doubt the persecution he and the early Church endured seemed to him to be the tribulation. Throughout the ages, each generation has seen its own tribulation and has thought, "This is the time of His coming." That is precisely why the revelation of the rapture and coming judgment was given! It is the "hope" of the Christian.[21]

Some people, looking at the past history of the Church, lose this hope and devalue the doctrine of the second coming. Peter prophesies that some will say, "Where is the promise of His coming? for since the fathers fell asleep, all things continue as they were from the beginning of the creation."[22] They surrender the hope because Jesus is hidden to them in the dark folds of the portrait of time. Yet His very obscureness is meant to keep the Church alert. He said:

Therefore keep watch, because you do not know on what day your Lord will come.[23]

It will be good for those servants whose master finds them ready, even if he comes in the second or third watch of the night.[24]

Be always on the watch, and pray that you may be able to escape all that is about to happen, and that you may be able to stand before the Son of Man.[25]

Every generation of Christians is to be prepared for the coming of the Lord. If men knew that He would not come during their lifetime, they might become lethargic in their Christian walk and witness. Why be concerned about world evangelism if the world has plenty of time? If, however, the end of time is near, and men will suffer the awfulness of the tribulation and the Day of the Lord without Christ, the Church has an inducement for outreach. The concept of a coming holocaust has motivated the Church throughout the ages.

The thought of standing before the Bridegroom has helped the Bride of Christ purify herself throughout the millenniums. Jesus told the Church, "Therefore be ye also ready: for in such an hour as ye think not the Son of man cometh;" and, "He that overcometh, the same shall be clothed in white raiment; and I will not blot out his name out of the book of life, but I will confess his name before My Father, and before His angels."[26] In times of great trials and great temptations, knowledge of the second coming of Christ, the judgment to come, and the promised rapture of the Church has inspired believers to live lives surrendered to the sanctifying work of the Holy Spirit. The anticipation created by the secrecy of His coming has helped in the preparation of the Bride.

In the ancient bridal customs of Israel, the bridegroom went to bring his bride to his home for the wedding festivities. The bride would receive a blessing from her family, such as the one received by Rebekah.

And they blessed Rebekah and said to her, "Our sister, may you increase to thousands upon thousands; may your offspring possess the gates of their enemies."[27]

The bride left her home adorned for her bridegroom as described by the prophet Ezekiel:

I adorned you with jewelry: I put bracelets on your arms and a necklace around your neck, and I put a ring on your nose, earrings on your ears and a beautiful crown on your head.[28]

While the streets of the city were dark, those in the bride's party carried lamps or torches. They lit the way to the bridegroom's house. The coming of the bridegroom for the bride was a time of joy and gladness.[29]

The bride knew the bridegroom was coming, and something about the anticipated time, but not the exact hour. The expectation of the bridegroom's coming heightened the excitement and joy of the occasion.

In the dark shadows of night within the painting, seven lights streak across its vista. They orbit a path in heaven, like lamps being carried through a dark city street. Their coming means destruction to a sinful humanity. A holocaust of horror comes from the bowls they bring to the wedding feast. In the eclipse of their coming, He lurks in concealment. He comes secretly to the home of the Bride on earth. But once He has her secure in His Father's house, He will reveal Himself as the bridegroom.

End Notes

1. Rev. 16:1;5. **2.** Rev. 15:5,8. **3.** Ex. 25:20; Heb. 13:2. **4.** Rev. 16:16. **5.** Ibid. **6.** Rev. 15:1. **7.** Obad. 15. **8.** Obad. 15 (NIV). **9.** Joel 1:15; 2:1-2; 10-11; 30-31 (NIV). **10.** Is. 13:6-13 (NIV). **11.** Zeph. 1:14-2:3 (NIV). **12.** Acts 2:19-20 (NIV). **13.** 2 Pet. 3:9-10 (NIV). **14.** Joel 3:14 (NIV). **15.** II Pet. 3:10. **16.** 1 Thess. 5:2 (NIV). **17.** Rev. 16:15. **18.** John 18:20 (NIV). **19.** Acts 1:7. **20.** I Thess. 4:17. **21.** I Thess. 2:19. **22.** II Pet. 3:4. **23.** Matt. 24:42 (NIV). **24.** Luke 12:38 (NIV). **25.** Luke 21:36 (NIV). **26.** Matt. 24:44; Rev. 3:5. **27.** Gen. 24:60 (NIV). **28.** Ezek. 16:11-12 (NIV). **29.** Jer. 7:34.

Portrait 9

The Bridegroom[*]

The next painting in the gallery of John's spirit suddenly changes from a portrait of revulsion, fright and damnation to a canvas filled with love, breathtaking beauty and joy. The background of the mural no longer depicts the trepidation of a world covered with the plagues of disease, famine, war and death. The contrast between the two paintings is startling. It is like turning a corner from a corridor draped in deep gray and purple shadows into a room filled with the bright colors of sunlight. The environment of the new portrait reveals the majesty of Heaven, resplendent with wholeness, bounty, love and life.

The subjects of the portrait are greatly changed. No longer are the faces of the witnesses of the tribulation

---

* Rev. 19:1-10.

twisted in agony. Gone are the hideous, shadowy, demonic forms. The garish figures of the brothel and its prostitute, arrayed in garments of purple and scarlet, have been removed with the solvent of the blood of the saints.[1] The central figure of the portrait is no longer a scarlet-colored beast with seven heads and ten horns.[2] Now a Lamb dressed in the robes of a royal Bridegroom is painted. The Lamb is ascending to the place of honor. Instead of a scarlet whore, a Bride stands next to the Lamb. She is dressed in fine white linen.[3] She is crowned with a tiara of jewels, indicating her victory over sin. Her form and visage are perfect. Her beauty rivals all of the radiance of Heaven. The faces of the witnesses reflect the joy of the wedding as they sit at a table as large as time and eternity. The wedding feast abounds with all things that please the spirit, soul and taste of men and angels.

The scene is painted in colors of brilliance. Indescribable glory radiates from every part of the mural. A voice speaks as we view the scene. It is a voice of power and authority, one that reminds the viewer of rushing water and rolling thunder in its intensity. But it cannot be the voice of God, for it calls the viewer to worship the omnipotent One. As we begin to prostrate ourselves before the voice, our attention is directed, by the voice, once more to the canvas. We are told, "Worship God; for the testimony of Jesus is the spirit of prophecy."[4] Will you join the artist, as we worship the One in the portrait of the marriage supper of the Lamb?

The Everlasting Feast

The Jewish wedding feast lasted seven days.[5] This seven-day period was symbolic, even though the Jewish people did not realize it, of the apocalyptic number seven. The feast is, therefore, complete and everlasting. The number of days of the feast are often confused with the seven-year duration of the tribulation. The Apocalypse does not exhibit the Church at the wedding feast for the span of the tribulation period. The tribulation period is divided by Daniel, and by John's revelation, into two periods of three and one-half years each—the latter being called "great tribulation."[6] The division tells us that the seven-year tribulation period is not an apocalyptic number, while the period of time in the Jewish wedding feast suggests apocalyptic completeness. All of the feasts of Israel are apocalyptic in nature, and the wedding feast of the Lamb is the ultimate "seven" of these highly symbolic feasts by which God teaches His way of salvation. The portrait of the wedding feast cannot be understood separate from the etchings, the feasts of Israel, that were used to create its colors and pageantry.

The Feasts of Israel

The Passover. God said to Israel:

For seven days you are to eat the bread made without yeast. On the first day remove the yeast from your houses, for whoever eats anything with yeast in it from the first day through the seventh must be cut off from Israel.[7]

The seven-day feast of the Passover is apocalyptic symbolism. A glass of salt water was placed on the table of the feast, recalling the bitter, salty tears of the Jews during their enslavement in Egypt, and illustrative of the Red Sea through which Israel passed. Three *matzos,* cakes of unleavened bread, reminded Israel of the speed with which God could deliver. The shank bone of the passover lamb and four cups of wine prompted remembrance of the blood of a lamb, sprinkled on the doorpost of every Jewish home when death passed over. A hard-boiled egg suggested the sacrifice. Bitter herbs jogged memories of the sorrow of slavery. The *charoseth,* a sauce made from apples and nuts, represented the clay with which the Jews were forced to make bricks for the pharaohs.

Jesus used the apocalyptic nature of the feast of the Passover to express His relationship to His Church:

...and when He had given thanks, He broke it and said, "This is My body, which is for you; do this in remembrance of Me." In the same way, after supper He took the cup, saying, "This cup is the new covenant in My blood; do this, whenever you drink it, in remembrance of Me."[8]

Jesus is the reality of what the apocalyptic symbolism of the Passover meant to communicate. He is the overcoming of death through the resurrection. He is the deliverance from the slavery of sin. Paul wrote of Jesus as the Christian's passover:

Get rid of the old yeast that you may be a new batch without yeast—as you really are. For Christ, our Passover Lamb, has been sacrificed. Therefore let us keep the Festival, not with the old yeast, the yeast of malice and wickedness, but with bread without yeast, the bread of sincerity and truth.[9]

Pentecost is the Greek word translated "fifty," by which the feast of weeks (*Shavuoth*) was designated, for it occurred 50 days after the Passover Sabbath. This was the thanksgiving celebration to God for the gathering of the wheat. Because the religious leaders of Israel believed that Moses presented the law to Israel on the Day of Pentecost, it was considered to be the birthday of the Jews. Pentecost was celebrated by Jewish families gathering for a meal. Two loaves of the finest bread were eaten, representing the two "wave-loaves" that were presented to God at the temple. Ripe figs, grapes and pomegranates (*bikkurim*) or firstfruits of the festival were included in the meal. During the celebration, the Book of Ruth was read.

During the celebration of Pentecost, the disciples of Jesus were baptized in the Holy Spirit.[10] Three thousand believers were added to Christianity as the spiritual firstfruits of the Church.

Rosh Hashana is basically a celebration of new beginnings. God commanded Moses:

Say to the Israelites: "On the first day of the seventh month you are to have a day of rest, a sacred assembly commemorated with trumpet blasts."[11]

According to the Book of Nehemiah, the celebration of *Rosh Hashana* was a solemn event.[12] The ram's horn brought memories of the substitution of a ram for Isaac.[13] The blowing of the horn called Israel to repentance, and reminded the Jewish people of their covenant relationship with God.

Christians have not been involved in the feasts of Israel since the feast day of Pentecost in Acts, chapter 2. Could the sounding of the trumpet, described by the apostle Paul in his first letter to the Thessalonians, be the equivalent of the feast of *Rosh Hashana?*

For the Lord Himself shall descend from heaven with a shout, with the voice of the archangel, and with the trump of God: and the dead in Christ shall rise first: then we which are alive and remain shall be caught up together with them in the clouds to meet the Lord in the air: and so shall we ever be with the Lord.[14]

If the trumpet which gathers the Church is equivalent to the trumpet of *Rosh Hashana,* the next event in the Church calendar is the rapture, or catching up of the Church to Heaven. If, however, *Rosh Hashana* is analogous to the seven trumpets of the Apocalypse, the next event for the Church is the tribulation.[15] Since God is preparing a Bride for a wedding feast, it seems unlikely that He would have her suffer His wrath. The Church is "not appointed...to wrath."[16] Christians "shall be saved from wrath."[17] Christians "are not in darkness, that that day should overtake [them] as a thief."[18] There is a continuing debate in the Church as to when the sounding of the trumpet and subsequent removal of the Church occurs, in relationship to the events of the end times. This one thing is certain: The Church will celebrate the feast of *Rosh Hashana*.

A feast of major importance to Israel is the feast of **Yom Kippur**. The words *Yom Kippur* mean " the Day of Atonement." A description of the event is recorded in the Book of Leviticus.

> *The priest who is anointed and ordained to succeed his father as high priest is to make atonement. He is to put on the sacred linen garments and make atonement for the Most Holy Place, for the Tent of Meeting and the altar, and for the priests and all the people of the community. "This is to be a lasting ordinance for you: Atonement is to be made once a year for all the sins of the Israelites.—) And it was done, as the Lord commanded Moses.[19]*

Atonement for sin and the Book of Life were aligned from the time of Moses.[20]The Jewish people bless each other with a prayer that they be sealed in the Book of

Life. This blessing is given before *Yom Kippur*, when the Book of Accounting is opened. So the judgment of the tribulation will be heaped upon those who have not received the atonement, and whose names are not written in the Lamb's Book of Life.

> *He was given power to make war against the saints and to conquer them. And he was given authority over every tribe, people, language and nation. All inhabitants of the earth will worship the beast—all whose names have not been written in the book of life belonging to the Lamb that was slain from the creation of the world.*[21]

The feast of Tabernacles, or Booths, is called **Succoth** in the Hebrew. The basis for *Succoth* is found in the Book of Leviticus:

> *So beginning with the fifteenth day of the seventh month, after you have gathered the crops of the land, celebrate the festival to the Lord for seven days; the first day is a day of rest, and the eighth day also is a day of rest. On the first day you are to take choice fruit from the trees, and palm fronds, leafy branches and poplars, and rejoice before the Lord your God for seven days. Celebrate this as a festival to the Lord for seven days each year. This is to be a lasting ordinance for the generations to come; celebrate it in the seventh month. Live in booths*

for seven days: All native-born Israelites are to live in booths so your descendants will know that I had the Israelites live in booths when I brought them out of Egypt. I am the Lord your God.[22]

Through the Feast of Tabernacles, Israel commemorates 40 years of living in tents. The booths were made of plaited branches called *lulav*. For six days, water was poured out in the temple as a visual sign of God's grace in sending rain. On the seventh day, *lulav* were waved in the temple with cries of "Hosanna!" John pictured the celebration of *Succoth* before Jesus in Heaven.

After this I looked and there before me was a great multitude that no one could count, from every nation, tribe, people and language, standing before the throne and in front of the Lamb. They were wearing white robes and were holding palm branches in their hands. And they cried out in a loud voice: "Salvation belongs to our God, who sits on the throne, and to the Lamb."[23]

Hanukkah is the feast of dedication, which Jesus celebrated by going to the temple.[24] The celebration memorializes the Jewish uprising, under Judas Maccabee, against the Syrians who had captured Jerusalem during the reign of Antiochus Epiphanes. Antiochus commanded that pigs be sacrificed on the holy altars of the Jews. After Judas Maccabee drove the Syrians out, the temple was rededicated. During the time of dedication, a cruse of oil that was sufficient for one night of lighting the temple lasted for eight days, while a new supply of oil was being consecrated. The miracle allowed the dedication of the temple to take place on *Kislev,* the 25th day of December, 164 B.C. On this day, light came into the world. Christians adopted this day to celebrate the coming of the "light of the world." We call it—Christmas.

Purim is the feast of Queen Esther. The book of the Bible named for her tells how Esther saved the nation of Israel from complete annihilation during the reign of Xerxes of Persia. Esther was chosen by Xerxes to be his bride without his knowing that she was a Jew.[25] At the urging of his prime minister Haman, Xerxes signed a decree to execute all of the Jews.[26] The timing of the decree was determined by casting lots. Esther requested that the king give a banquet and that he invite Haman. At the banquet, Esther confronted Xerxes with Haman's plot, and with the information that the king's decree would have Esther put to death.

Xerxes, angry at the way he had been tricked, left the banquet and went into the palace garden. While Xerxes was gone, Haman laid down on a couch next to Esther.[27] When Xerxes returned to the room, he decided that Haman had exceeded his privileges as prime minister, and commanded that Haman be hanged upon the gallows built for Mordecai, the leader of the Jews. Xerxes also gave permission for the Jews to defend themselves against their enemies. The day of the decree is called the celebration of *pur,* after the casting of lots.

The banquet of Esther, the bride queen, is representative of the wedding supper of the Lamb and His Bride/Queen—the Church! After the wedding feast, the devil will be cast from Heaven into a lake of fire and brimstone, and tormented forever.[28]

Preparing for the Wedding

Each of the pre-*purim* feasts of Israel are illustrative of a step in the Christian's preparation for the wedding of the Lamb. Passover depicts the salvation experience. It is the shed blood of Calvary applied to the heart of the believer by faith that gives eternal life, and thus the passing over of eternal death. Passover implies a union between the Christ and the believer in which the believer dies with Christ, the Lamb, in order to live with Christ, the Lord. The apostle Paul wrote:

> *I have been crucified with Christ and I no longer live, but Christ lives in me. The life I live in the body, I live by faith in the Son of God, who loved me and gave Himself for me.*[29]

Pentecost represents baptism in the fires of sanctification which purify the Christian from the sins forgiven on the cross. It is the work of the Holy Spirit to sanctify the believer.[30] Although sanctification is a life-long process, it has its beginning in the baptism in the Holy Spirit. Paul said of the Christians justified on the cross:

And that is what some of you were. But you were washed, you were sanctified, you were justified in the name of the Lord Jesus Christ and by the spirit of our God.[31]

Rosh Hashana deals with the resurrection of the body. Paul wrote:

I declare to you, brothers, that flesh and blood cannot inherit the kingdom of God, nor does the perishable inherit the imperishable. Listen, I tell you a mystery: We will not all sleep, but we will all be changed—in a flash, in the twinkling of an eye, at the last trumpet. For the trumpet will sound, the dead will be raised imperishable, and we will be changed. For the perishable must clothe itself with the imperishable, and the mortal with immortality. When the perishable has been clothed with the imperishable, and the mortal with immortality, then the saying that is written will come true: "Death has been swallowed up in victory."[32]

Since "flesh and blood cannot inherit the kingdom of God," and at the sound of "the trumpet" the Christian will go through a type of metamorphosis from the physical into the spiritual, all disciples of Christ will be called by the trumpet of *Rosh Hashana.*

Likewise, all Christians will also stand at the "judgment seat of Christ."[33] There, the Book of Life will be opened as on the day of *Yom Kippur*.[34] Atonement for the Christian has already occurred—on the cross.[35] The Christian will not be judged by his works, but his works will be evaluated.[36]

The Bride of Christ has a wedding gown prepared for her bridal feast. It was provided by justification and washed in sanctification. The Bride is warned, however, to make sure she is clothed in white raiment, lest she be shamed.[37] The Bridegroom is expecting a Bride dressed in a wedding garment of such purity:

> *That He might present it to Himself a glorious church, not having spot, or wrinkle, or any such thing; but that it should be holy and without blemish.*[38]

The Wedding Party

The participants of a wedding party are fairly standard. There must be a bride and groom and, of course, one can usually find a best man and bridesmaids. There also can be wedding guests.

The bride is the focus of all weddings. All eyes turn to the bride as she enters the wedding chapel. The scene has been created to emphasize her grace and radiance. The groom and his attendants may be dressed in black, the bridesmaids in color, but the bride is always in startling white. For her and her alone the wedding service has been formed. This hour will legitimize her love. This hour will elevate her position. This hour will give her authority in the household. After the wedding night, she will no longer be a maid in waiting, but the wife and mistress of the house.

To certify her new position, the Jewish bridegroom presented his wife with a wedding banquet immediately after his declaration of marriage. At the banquet, the bride took her place at the head of the table with him. They shared a cup together, and all present recognized her lofty place with him.

The Bride in the painting is the Church. She is adorned in a gown of pure white.[39] She receives from Him the chalice—the same cup they had shared together spiritually on the earth.[40] Now she watches Him "face to face" and drinks of the wine through which she has been, and now is, exalted.[41]

The Christ of the Apocalypse in the wedding picture is painted in the figure of a Lamb-Bridegroom. He is a Lamb because the cup He offers His Bride is the cup of His sacrifice on the altar of the cross. He is a Bridegroom, not clothed in the costume of an earthly bridegroom, but arrayed with a brilliance and splendor that rivals that of His Bride. He is the Lamb, but He is also a royal Bridegroom!

The best man in a Jewish wedding was also called the "friend of the bridegroom." John the Baptist gave witness that Jesus was the Bridegroom and that he, John, was the "friend of the bridegroom."[42] It was John who announced, "Behold the Lamb of God, which taketh away the sin of the world."[43] As the friend, John announced the approach of the bridegroom.

Jesus told a story about the bridesmaids. He said that the bride had ten, (the biblical number for completeness) virgins or maids in attendance. The parable of the ten virgins is not directed to the church, but to Israel. Jesus is not a polygamist! The Lord Jesus Christ does not have a group of churches. There will be no Baptist, Catholic, Presbyterian, Methodist or Pentecostal churches in the Kingdom of God. There is only one Church—one Bride![44] Jesus does not have a Bride who is missing half of her body. The Bride does not have to "buy" the oil of the Holy Spirit.[45] It was Israel under the law that had to purchase her salvation; the Bride is saved by grace![46] The bridesmaids (Jews), however, who have purchased their oil and used it well, will attend the wedding as guests.

A wedding is a joyous occasion. It is a special event. To signify its uniqueness, the participants clothe themselves in special attire. Isaiah said that the bridegroom was arrayed with "ornaments" and the bride with "jewels."[47] Ezekiel described the bride as being "girded... with fine linen, and...covered...with silk."[48] She had "bracelets" on her hands, "a chain" on her neck, "a jewel on [her] forehead," and was "decked with gold and silver...and broidered work."[49] Those invited to the wedding would also adorn themselves for the glorious procession through the streets.

Jesus told a story about a man who dared attend a wedding without proper apparel. He said:

But when the king came in to see the guests, he noticed a man there who was not wearing wedding clothes. "Friend," he asked, "how did you get in here without wedding clothes?" The man was speechless. Then the king told the attendants, "Tie him hand and foot, and throw him outside, into the darkness, where there will be weeping and gnashing of teeth." For many are invited, but few are chosen.[50]

The wedding garments are coverings of righteousness. Jesus warned, "Behold, I come as a thief. Blessed is he that watcheth, and keepth his garments, lest he walk naked, and they see his shame."[51]

The Coming Wedding

What a splendid painting! This mural that transfixed itself into the mind and spirit of John was filled with the colors of pageantry. The canvas incorporated all of the feasts of Israel and all of the purpose of history. The picture also displays design. Events on earth are not continuing haphazardly. History is being orchestrated. Events are flowing in a pattern. Each feast of Israel is materializing in order. As surely as the Jewish Passover was followed by the Day of Pentecost, the Lamb offered (Jesus on Calvary) is followed by the event of the Holy Spirit (the New Testament Pentecost). All of history is preparing for a wedding!

The Bridegroom is dressed in His best royal attire. He paces the portal of His heavenly palace, awaiting with great patience the preparation of His Bride. He has a royal chamber prepared for her. His best man watches from the side of the court, as he anticipates the delight of his friend when the Bride comes. The wedding table is set with the finest of crystal, gold and silver. Foods to remind the Bride of her perilous journey from the darkness of sin to the light of glory abound.

Now the Church-Bride is seen in the portrait. She comes to the wedding feast arrayed in garments of brilliant white righteousness, without spot or wrinkle. The central figure in the painting is still the Christ of the Apocalypse. His magnificence dominates the portrait. His splendor overshadows the breathtaking vista of His heavenly home. His magisterial radiance outshines the brilliance of the jewels, the opulence of the table, and the vivid pigments in the mural. Yet, when the viewer studies the portrait and centers on the Christ, the most remarkable truth comes to light—the Christ of the Apocalypse has eyes only for the beauty of the Bride!

End Notes

1. Rev. 17:4-6. 2. Rev. 17:3. 3. Rev. 19:8. 4. Rev. 19:10. 5. Judg. 14:17. 6. Rev. 2:22. 7. Ex. 12:15 (NIV). 8. 1 Cor. 11:24-25 (NIV). 9. 1 Cor. 5:7-8 (NIV). 10. Acts 2. 11. Lev. 23:24 (NIV). 12. Neh. 8:1-12. 13. Gen. 22:13. 14. I Thess. 4:16-17. 15. Rev. 8:2; Matt. 24:21,29. 16. I Thess. 5:9. 17. Rom. 5:9. 18. I Thess. 5:4. 19. Lev. 16:32-34. 20. Ex. 32:30-32. 21. Rev. 13:7-8 (NIV). 22. Lev. 23:39-43 (NIV). 23. Rev. 7:9-10. 24. John 10:22-23. 25. Esther 2:17. 26. Esther 3:12. 27. Esther 7:8. 28. Rev. 20:10. 29. Gal. 2:20 (NIV). 30. Rom. 15:16. 31. 1 Cor. 6:11 (NIV). 32. 1*Cor. 15:50-54 (NIV)*. 33. Rom. 14:10. 34. Rev. 13:8. 35. Rom. 5:11. 36. Rev. 14:13. 37. Rev. 3:18. 38. Eph. 5:27. 39. Ibid. 40. Luke 22:18. 41. I Cor. 13:12. 42. John 3:29. 43. John 1:29. 44. Eph. 4:5. 45. Matt. 25:9. 46. Eph. 2:8. 47. Isa. 61:10. 48. Ezek. 16:10. 49. Ezek. 16:11-13. 50. Matt. 22:11-14 (NIV). 51. Rev. 16:15.

Portrait 10

The Judge*

Have you seen the judgment paintings in the hall of the Apocalypse? The next painting, titled "The Judge," is not at all like those found in the other wings of the gallery. The others depict the great white throne of judgment! Sitting on the throne is the Creator of the universe. His face is forbidding and radiates with judgment. Before the judgment throne stand the multitudes. The expressions on their faces are defiant. They openly accuse God of false judgment. They parade what they think are their good points. They call the Truth a lie, and falsehood truth. Their insolence does not do them any good in the light of the revelation of their hearts, for the fires of eternal death and separation from the only Source of life already blaze. Everlasting

---

*   Rev. 20:4-6.

death and eternal hell are their pronounced judgment. There is no Christ in those paintings.

The painting called "The Judge," which hangs in the gallery of the Christ, is not painted with the contrasting color of the white throne against the deep reds and bright oranges of the flames of hell. This mural reveals an event with which John was familiar.

Elders often sat in judgment at the gates of a city. This was the Jews' custom during the period of the Judges of Israel, and the custom was handed down through the generations. In the portrait seen by John's spirit, the gates of the city are expanded to encompass the world. Thrones are placed in the immense gates that symbolize all of the peoples, nations and cities of the world. Sitting on one of the thrones is the Christ of the Apocalypse. He is dressed as John had seen Him so many times. John paints Him in the simple robe of the rabbi—white homespun with a hem of blue. On ten of the other thrones John has portrayed his closest friends—the apostles. If you look closely at the images of the men sitting on the thrones, you will see that the artist painted a self-portrait upon one of them.

Before the thrones, John portrayed people from every time and culture—from primeval man to the astronauts. Before the occupied 12 thrones of the apostles he painted every generation of the 12 tribes of Israel. Before the judgment throne of Christ he sketched the Church, made up of people from every culture and nation. Some of the saints wear crowns of pure gold. The crowns of others sparkle with breathtaking jewels. Still others carry scepters, signifying rulership over cities or territories. Some are portrayed as being bewildered at the lavishness of the treasure that surrounds their feet. Their faces, unlike the defiant looks of those depicted in the painting of the great white throne, are sketched as having expressions of gratitude, humility and surprise.

The face of Jesus, in the portrait, is filled with pleasure. He looks like someone who has given a gift and is acquiring joy and anticipation from watching the loved one receive the gift. His countenance fairly explodes with delight, as each child of God receives the rewards of his faithfulness. John depicts the Lord of Heaven as watching intently the face of the recipient as each honor is given. When the one encountering the blessing questions his worthiness to receive the tribute given, the viewer can imagine Jesus breaking into a tooth-filled grin and shouting, "I tell you the truth, whatever you did for one of the least of these brothers of Mine, you did for Me."[1]

There is no envy or jealousy painted in the countenances of those receiving. Although one receives more than another, according to their words and faithfulness, each is shown rejoicing over the other's great fortune. Their joy at seeing each other blessed and honored is rivalled only by the ecstasy in the face of the One giving the judgment. The viewer recognizes that no one in the painting would complain, "That is my gift—I deserved that!" As each of them receive their reward, they look in wonder and amazement. The faces in the painting reveal that the blessed would protest their unworthiness, except for their knowledge of the sheer joy that Jesus is receiving from giving the gifts.

Notice the festive, exciting brightness of the colors! John's painting of the judgment seat of Christ is one of bright colors and gaiety. It is filled with hilarity, exhilaration and mirth. One can almost hear the gates of the city ringing with the sounds of glee and laughter. It is like Christmas morning, the Fourth of July and a birthday party, all rolled into one. The children of God are having a celebration at the place of judgment, and the Christ of the Apocalypse is the One enjoying it most of all!

The Book of Life

One becomes a Christian by grace through faith, not by works.[2] The judgment of the great white throne is for the works of those who have not received Jesus Christ as Lord and Savior. When individuals receive Christ into their lives, they receive eternal life itself. Jesus is the Life! The Book of Life is the record of those to whom He has given life. If a name is not found in this book, the judgment is implicit. Guilt of neglecting God's great salvation is already established, and only the pronouncement of the judgment remains at the throne. John wrote:

Then I saw a great white throne and Him who was seated on it. Earth and sky fled from His presence, and there was no place for them. And I saw the dead, great and small, standing before the throne, and books were opened. Another book was opened, which is the book of life. The dead were judged according to what they had done as recorded in the books. The sea gave up the dead that were in it, and death and Hades gave up the dead that were in them, and each person was judged according to what he had done. Then death and Hades were thrown into the lake of fire. The lake of fire is the second death. If anyone's name was not found written in the book of life, he was thrown into the lake of fire.[3]

The true Christian need never fear the lake of fire, where death and hell are. Eternal death is the penalty of sin, but Jesus, on the cross, died in the place of the sinner and fulfilled the law. Those united with Christ in His death on the cross are united with Him in His life in the resurrection. When one is "born again," he is born into "eternal" life. That which is eternal can never end. So long as the Christian looks to the Christ for redemption, his name is written in the Lamb's Book of Life. Jesus promises the Christian:

He who overcomes will, like them, be dressed in white. I will never blot out his name from the book of life, but will acknowledge his name before My Father and His angels.[4]

The Christian will not be judged at the great white throne judgment, for only the "dead" are there, and although a Christian can be "absent from the body," the child of God is eternally alive.[5]

The Thrones of Judgment

Jesus told the apostles:

I tell you the truth, at the renewal of all things, when the Son of Man sits on His glorious throne, you who have followed Me will also sit on twelve thrones, judging the twelve tribes of Israel.[6]

Salvation comes to the Jew the same way it comes to the Gentile—by grace. God has not turned His back on Israel. But all Israel are not of Israel! Paul wrote:

It is not as though God's word had failed. For not all who are descended from Israel are Israel. Nor because they are his descendants are they all Abraham's children. On the contrary, "It is through Isaac that your offspring will be reckoned." In other words, it is not the natural children who are God's children, but it is the children of the promise who are regarded as Abraham's offspring.[7]

It is not natural Israel that God promised to save, but a remnant made righteous.[8] The remnant of Israel that will be before the thrones of the apostles are those Jews who received the election of grace and did not trust in works.[9] They will be rewarded for their works, but not judged by their works!

The Judgment Throne of Christ

Paul wrote concerning the Church:

For we must all appear before the judgment seat of Christ, that each one may receive what is due him for the things done while in the body, whether good or bad.[10]

Many see the judgment seat of Christ as something to be feared—expecting punishment for the "bad" things they did while on the earth. All "bad" things are sin, and all sin was paid for on the cross! Not only is sin forgiven, sin also is forgotten.[11] God's grace is a perfect grace. Grace forgets! It would be against God's character for Him to keep a record of sins He has forgiven. If He did have such a book, it would be blank—for the sins of the Christian have been eradicated by the blood of Jesus Christ. Paul is speaking about various degrees of, or lack of, reward. He continues to say that since Christians know what the "terror of the Lord" is (toward sinners, not His children), we "persuade men."[12] The terror of the Lord is an inducement to evangelism, not an incitement for fear. The Christian who wins others to Christ will be rewarded with a crown at the coming of the Lord.[13]

There will be differences in the rewards given to God's children. Paul wrote to Christians, saying:

If any man builds on this foundation using gold, silver, costly stones, wood, hay or straw, his work will be shown for what it is, because the Day will bring it to light. It will be revealed with fire, and the fire will test the quality of each man's work. If what he has built survives, he will receive his reward. If it is burned up, he will suffer loss; he himself will be saved...[14]

Jesus indicated in His parables that there were degrees of reward. In the parable of the talents, He related how one steward received two talents and another five, as a reward for their faithfulness.[15] In the parable of the workers called into the harvest, Jesus stated that the amount of the reward was to be decided by the Lord of the harvest.[16]

Paul reveals that various crowns will be given for distinct services to the Lord. There is a crown for those with temperance, a crown for those who look in love for His second coming, a crown for the man who endures temptation, a crown for those who shepherd the flock of God, and a crown for those who suffer even unto death for the sake of the gospel.[17]

There could be no jealousy, envy or resentment among those receiving the crowns of reward, since the gifts are given to a perfected Church. There could be no punishment or penalty received, nor any anguish or humiliation felt by the Bride, at the judgment seat of Christ. The portrait of the judgment seat comes in the gallery of the Revelation after the depiction of the wedding. A bridegroom does not reproach his bride on their honeymoon. No! He showers her with gifts!

End Notes

1. Matt. 25:40 (NIV). **2.** Eph. 2:8. **3.** Rev. 20:11-15 (NIV). **4.** Rev. 3:5 (NIV). **5.** Rev. 20:12; II Cor. 5:8. **6.** Matt. 19:28 (NIV). **7.** Rom. 9:6-8 (NIV). **8.** Rom 9:27-28. **9.** Rom. 11:5-6. **10.** 2 Cor. 5:10 (NIV). **11.** Ps. 103:12. **12.** II Cor. 5:11. **13.** II Tim. 4:8. **14.** 1 Cor. 3:12-15 (NIV). **15.** Matt. 25:14-23. **16.** Matt. 20:15. **17.** I Cor. 9:25; II Tim. 4:8; James 1:12; I Pet. 5:2; Rev. 2:10.

Portrait 11

The Word of God[*]

White-capped waves cresting the blue sea slapped against the rocks of the island's shore line. John was both enraptured and disturbed by the visions that had paraded across his soul. In the dark, foreboding, storm-filled canvases of tribulation he had also seen the glory of his Lord and friend, Jesus. He experienced to some degree the happiness of his friend's wedding. Even if he could not worship Jesus in person, he had attempted to show his devotion by worshiping the angel of prophecy.

The next portrait came out of the essence of John's spirit. In the painting, the dark blue of the heavens roll back to reveal a warrior riding upon a great white

------

*   Rev. 19:11-21.

horse. Following the warrior, like Roman legions in battle array, are brigades of a horse cavalry. The colors of the battle flags contrast sharply with the army itself. The soldiers are all dressed in white. Like their leader, all ride upon horses that look as if they had been carved from the purest ivory.

The commander of the horsemen has diadem upon jeweled diadem on his head. The golden, gem-covered crowns flash like the rays of the sun as he rides through the heavens. However, the glitter upon his head is pallid compared to the flash of fire from his eyes. Like the blaze from a torch, his eyes send rays of fire, searching out his enemies. From his open mouth the viewer can almost hear a battle cry. His words form the shape of a sharp sword. The saber of his word is the only weapon John paints in the entire portrait!

As the conqueror is viewed by looking upward at the painting, one can see that the purity of his white dress is spotted with the deep crimson color of blood. Across his chestplate and down his thigh, the viewer also can see that John has painted chevrons indicating the conqueror's station and rank. He is the King of Kings and Lord of Lords!

A gold nameplate in the frame identifies the portrait as being that of *"The Word of God!"*

The Mighty Warrior

Did you see the portrait of Jesus painted by Matthew? The one of Jesus as a babe born in a stable? As the suffering Lamb, a stable was appropriate! When Jesus returns to this earth, John no longer sees Him as the meek Lamb, but as a Mighty Warrior. No longer will Jesus be taken to the cross. Who would dare attempt to capture, humiliate and treat Him as a common slave? When a Roman general had a triumph, he was brought through the streets on a white steed. Christ has already won His victory, so He presents Himself upon the white horse of triumph and rides with splendor through the arch of the heavens. The battle flags of the Church are unfurled and the saints ride behind their Commander-in-chief on white horses. This portrait does not depict a battle as much as it announces a parade! In a Roman's triumph, prisoners were brought to Rome for judgment. The word of the general who won the battle sealed their fate. Futhermore, it takes at least two fighting armies to make a battle. John wrote:

Then I saw three evil spirits that looked like frogs; they came out of the mouth of the dragon, out of the mouth of the beast and out of the mouth of the false prophet. They are spirits of demons performing miraculous signs, and they go out to the kings of the whole world, to gather them for the battle on the great day of God Almighty. "Behold, I come like a thief! Blessed is he who stays awake and keeps his clothes with him, so that he may not go naked and be shamefully exposed." Then they gathered the kings together to the place that in Hebrew is called Armageddon.[1]

John painted the armies of the world coming together to fight a battle at Armageddon. In this painting, he discloses the Mighty Warrior coming to Armageddon to celebrate His triumph. The armies of the world are prepared to fight with all weaponry—tanks, planes, rockets and biological and nuclear instruments of destruction. Jesus is pictured in the mural as dressed in royal court attire and riding a parade horse. The Church attends Him as an honor escort, on similar horses, carrying unfurled banners. The world may have come to fight a battle, but He has come to declare a victory! He comes as "The Word of God."[2]

As the Word, He is God.[3] As the Word, He created the heavens and the earth in an instant, before He created time.[4] As the Word, He released the spirit of God to activate the creation. Also as the Word, He releases His one weapon—the Sword!

The Sword of God

The sword of the Lord is the action of the Holy Spirit.[6] One of Jesus' purposes in coming was to bring the sword to the earth. Jesus said:

Do not suppose that I have come to bring peace to the earth. I did not come to bring peace, but a sword.[7]

What sword did He bring? When the apostle Peter drew his weapon in defense of the Lord, Jesus rebuked him and told Peter that "all who draw the sword will die by the sword."[8] When Jesus was carried to the cross, He could have resisted and called His disciples or His angels into combat, but He did not call for a physical sword.

There is only one recorded instance in the New Testament where the Church acted to bring about death. Ananias and his wife Sapphira had sold a possession and then lied to Peter and the disciples, claiming to have given all of the money as an offering. Peter pronounced judgment on the pair and they instantly forfeited their lives. Peter declared that their sin was that they had lied to the "Holy Ghost."[9] Peter did not wield the sword that took the spirits from Ananias and Sapphira; the Holy Ghost did!

When Gideon faced the armies of the Midianites, it was neither their numbers nor the power of Israel that won the battle. Gideon commanded:

When I blow with a trumpet, I and all that are with me, then blow ye the trumpets also on every side of all the camp, and say, The sword of the Lord, and of Gideon.[10]

Before the contest the Lord told Gideon, "I have delivered it into thine hand."[11] Like Christ at Armageddon, there was no battle. The men of Gideon spoke the word and let their light shine. The enemy army committed suicide. When the Spirit of God wields the sword, there is nothing else to do! Death, however, is not an escape; the judgment of His sword does not stop with death. Defeat at Armageddon is not the end of His sword of judgment. There are still the fires of hell for the antichrist and the false prophet, and the rule under a rod of iron for those who did not oppose Him but who never bowed before Him!

The Blood

In John's portrait of the Word of God, Jesus is splattered once more with blood. The blood is not, in this painting, the saving Blood on Calvary; it is the blood of those who oppose His rule. It is interesting to note that the major supplementary accents in this depiction of the Christ of the Apocalypse are those of the Word, the sword, and the blood. Those following the mighty Warrior on their own white horses are in the painting because they believed the Word, allowed the Spirit to apply the sword and are covered by the Blood. The only separation between those riding in the triumph and those condemned by the triumph is the Word of God—the Christ of the Apocalypse.

For we are to God the aroma of Christ among those who are being saved and those who are perishing. To the one we are the smell of death; to the other, the fragrance of life.[12]

End Notes

1. Rev. 16:13-16 (NIV). **2.** Rev. 19:13. **3.** John 1:1. **4.** John 1:3. **5.** Gen. 1:2. **6.** Eph. 6:17. **7.** Matt. 10:34 (NIV). **8.** Matt. 26:52 (NIV). **9.** Acts 5:1-11. **10.** Judg. 7:18. **11.** Judg. 7:9. **12.** 2 Cor. 2:15-16 (NIV).

Portrait 12

The King of Kings and Lord of Lords[*]

This painting is one of blackness, as if the canvas chosen was made from black velvet. The pigments placed upon the background of darkness are startling in their vividness. The coloring appears to be effervescent. In the very top of the painting we see the blue light of judgment being poured from a golden vial. In the glow of the luminescent blue light, a monster is revealed. It is a beast painted in lucid scarlet. Seven heads weave from the trunk of the creature. From the

------

*   Rev. 17:1-6; 19:11.

seven heads protrude ten horns, similar to the horns of a unicorn.

Riding on this hideous brute is an obese woman. Her corpulent frame is covered with rich attire, painted in brilliant colors of purple and scarlet. Around her portly neck hang chains of gold, precious stones and pearls in ostentatious numbers. Her pudgy fingers are enveloped in golden rings and flashing jewels. In her hand she holds a basin-sized golden chalice, from which she is pictured as perpetually drinking. The cup is filled with a noxious brew of blood, flesh and corruption. As she drinks from the cup, John's brush makes the concoction drip from her jaws. The artist shows that she is staggering. The woman depicted in the painting is drunk on the abominable mixture!

In startling contrast to the scarlet and blue coloring of the woman on the beast is another figure in the painting. A warrior dressed in white rides upon a pure white horse. The sharp sword that he wielded against the nations in the earlier painting still flashes from his mouth as a golden light. Now it is pointed at the woman and at the beast on which she rides. A name has been inscribed by the artist on the forehead of the opulent woman: "Mystery, Babylon the Great, the Mother of Harlots and Abominations of the Earth." The same brush also engraves a title across the breast and down the legs of the Rider of the white horse. He is *"The King of Kings and Lord of Lords!"*

The World System

The prophecies of Daniel are apocalyptic. Daniel interpreted several apocalyptic dreams. King Nebuchadnezzar dreamed of an apocalyptic image. It had a head of gold, breast and arms of silver, belly and thighs of brass, legs of iron, and ten toes that were part iron and part clay.[1] Daniel interpreted the dream as being the empire systems of the world. The colossus' gold head was the Babylonian Empire of Nebuchadnezzar. The silver arms were proven to be the Media-Persian Empire. The belly and thighs of brass are recognized as the Greek Empire. The legs of iron became the two sections of the Roman Empire, Rome and Constantinople.

Under the reign of Belshazzar of Babylon, Daniel had another apocalyptic vision. He saw a beast similar to a lion that had wings of an eagle; a creature similar to a bear that had three ribs in its mouth; an animal similar to a leopard, except that it had the wings of a bird; and a monster with iron teeth, that had ten horns on its head.[2]

Once again Daniel is describing, in apocalyptic terms, the world empire system. The sign of Babylon was the winged lion. Babylon, Media and Persia were devoured in the mouth of the Media-Persian Empire. Alexander the Great moved across the civilized world with the speed of a four-winged leopard, and the iron legions of Rome marched across the known world!

The similarity between the dream of Nebuchadnezzar, the vision of Daniel, and the apocalyptic painting of John is found in the number ten. Nebuchadnezzar's statue had ten toes, Daniel's fourth beast had ten horns, and John's revelation of the beast ridden by the scarlet woman painted the creature with ten horns. Nebuchadnezzar was a world dictator who established an empire. Likewise, Darius the Mead, Alexander the Great, and the Caesars of Rome were all dictators over empires. Nebuchadnezzar's colossus was to be destroyed by the Kingdom of God when it had ten toes, and the King of Kings and Lord of Lords will destroy the beast of dictatorship and world dominion with the sword of His mouth when a ten-nation confederacy has been established for world domination.[3]

The ten-nation confederacy will be made up "part of iron and part of clay."[4] The word used by Daniel and translated as "clay" is the Hebrew *chacaph*, which can mean a clod of earth, dirt or sand. The iron legs and toes of the colossus definitely referred to the Roman Empire with its two world centers, Rome and Constantinople. Constantinople was declared the capital of the Holy Roman Empire by Constantine in A.D. 330, but in A.D. 1453 the Ottomans captured Constantinople and replaced the cross of the Roman Empire with the crescent of Islam.

The sand (clay) empire of Daniel's colossus of the world empire systems could be none other than the Ottoman Empire. The Ottoman Empire consisted of Asia Minor, Greece, Bulgaria, Romania, parts of Hungary and Russia, Iraq, Syria, Palestine, Egypt, Arabia and

North Africa. Although the zenith of the sane empire was in A.D. 1566, it did not officially cease to exist until the end of World War I, with the formation of the republic of Turkey.

John wrote concerning the beast:

And here is the mind which hath wisdom. The seven heads are seven mountains, on which the woman sitteth.[5]

Because the city of Rome sits on seven hills and because the legs of the beast were of iron, many have mistakenly considered the beast to be Rome or the Roman Catholic Church.

However, the language is not realistic but apocalyptic! David used the word *mountain* apocalyptically, as meaning his kingdom.[6] Jeremiah used "mountain" apocalyptically, as referring to the kingdom of Babylon.[7] Daniel's interpretation of the dream of Nebuchadnezzar called the stone that became a great mountain the "Kingdom of God."[8] Of the seven mountains, John is told, "Five are fallen, and one is, and the other is not yet come."[9] Before John's time, there had been five empire kingdoms: Egypt, Assyria, Babylon, Persia and Greece. John lived in the empire that existed—Rome. Since John was in the Roman Empire, the beast could not be Rome. Rather, it is the empire system of which Rome is a part. Daniel saw fewer empire systems, but he started counting with the empires that existed during his time. John looked both forward and backward, and saw seven world powers. Out of these seven world powers will come a kingdom made up of a confederacy of ten dictators. This confederacy will control the earth for a short period of time.[10] This confederacy will be a binding of the iron (Roman culture) and sand (Arab culture) powers. They will have the economic dominion of the common Market and OPEC nations combined. The world will once more see Persia (Iraq and Iran) aligned with the nations of Europe and the nations of Russia. The alignment will not be one of organization, for iron cannot adhere to clay. It will, however, be an accommodation brought about by economic, political and military necessity.[11] The confederation will see a common enemy: Israel and the Kingdom of God!

During this period of time, when the European nations and the Russian nations are greatly involved with the Arab nations, the Kingdom of God will fall like a great rock from Heaven and crush the empire system![12]

The Whore

John saw a woman dressed in purple and scarlet clothing riding on the beast of the world empire system. She was embellished with jewelry and wore a crown upon which the name "Mystery, Babylon the Great, the Mother of Prostitutes, and the Abominations of the Earth" appeared.[13]

In the Scriptures, the words "harlot" or "prostitute," when used apocalyptically, refer to idol worship.[14]

Nimrod built a ziggurat (tower) in Babylon for the worship of the idol god, Marduk.[15] The name of the city of Babylon became synonymous with idolatry and disobedience. It was Babylon that captured God's people and held them captive.[16] It was Babylon that gave birth to the religion of ritual and sacrifices. The name of Babylon is a "mystery" because of the secret rituals and rites involved in the mystery religions. The beast on which the whore rides is the imperial systems existing since Nimrod.

The prostitute is not an empire; she rides upon empires, kings and dictators and controls them, but is superior to them. She does not rule with force, as do the despots of the empires, but controls with the seduction of her fornication. Empires come and go but the woman rides throughout all history. She rides on all of the seven-headed beasts. All seven (complete) world powers lift the whore as if she were their pride and joy. The governments of the world are the whore's servants and she is regarded as a most honorable lady!

The prostitute is not the Roman Catholic Church, for the prostitute was born before Christianity and will exist on earth until the judgment. She has been associated with Rome because of the roman imperial system, but she also could be identified with Babylon, Greece, Persia, Assyria and Egypt—all which existed before Rome. Nimrod intertwined the worship of idols with the power of his reign; the Egyptian priests were prized by the pharaohs; Assyria was filled with temples to the idol gods' and Greece and Rome worshiped so many idols that Paul even found a statue to the "unknown god" at Mars Hill.[17] History proves that the harlot of spiritual idolatry has ridden whenever a despotic rulership has reigned on earth. There is no separation of religion and government in the world empire system. The beast is controlled by the whore of ritual, works and sacrificial religion. Even as Islam rides the sand empire of the oil nations, the revised Roman empire is ridden by idolatrous spiritualism.

The secular, materialistic world society, however, will become more and more disillusioned with the fat and rich opulence of ritualistic, idolatrous religion. Government will turn on the whore who has ridden it so many ages, and will take away her riches and strip her of her purple and scarlet robes; thus, all will see her true nature. Government will devour her wealth and bring her to total social and political ruin. It is fitting that it is not the Christ of the Apocalypse who demolishes the whore of false religion, but the very tyrannical beast that kept her useful in ensnaring the souls of men. Jesus did not judge an adulterous woman when He was on earth, but He did bring judgment on those who would judge her.[18] He allows the kingdoms of the world to judge false religion, but the Kingdom of God judges the kingdoms of the world!

The Stone Cut Without Hands

Jesus came to build a kingdom. Since the concept of "kingdom" requires absolute loyalty to a lord, only one true kingdom can exist at a time. The kingdoms of this world must be replaced by the Kingdom of God. The sword of Christ, who is the white knight riding on the white horse, must slay the seven-headed monstrosity that represents the empire systems of this world.

Daniel saw the Kingdom of God as a mountain that fell on the goliath that represented the world empire system.[19] The Kingdom of the God of Heaven was a stone "cut out of the mountain without hands."[20] Thus Daniel indicates that the Kingdom of God can be neither formed nor created by man. The virgin birth of Jesus Christ is an absolute necessity if the prophecy of Daniel is true. Jesus had to be born without man, and He had to create a kingdom that man cannot develop or bring into existence.

Jesus related to the kingdom in two ways. He preached both a present kingdom and a coming kingdom. Wherever the king is present, the kingdom is at hand—now! The full reign of Jesus Christ over all creation will be established by His kingdom which is to come!

John the Baptist came preaching, "Repent ye: for the kingdom of heaven is at hand"; this is the realized kingdom now.[21] Jesus also preached that the Kingdom of Heaven was present.[22] The fact of His power over sickness, seen through His healing ministry, was evidence that the Kingdom was on the earth.[23] Yet, Jesus taught His disciples to pray, "Thy kingdom come. Thy will be done in earth, as it is in heaven."[24] His presence and His miracles were evidence of the realized kingdom; His prayer was for the coming eschatological kingdom.

The apostle Paul taught that the "kingdom of god is not meat and drink; but righteousness, and peace, and joy in the Holy Ghost."[25] He was speaking of the realized kingdom of the now; the kingdom that could be enjoyed by grace in his own time. Paul also looked for the second coming of Christ, when He would establish His universal rulership.[26]

Jesus promised His Church that, during the millennium, the Church would rule with Him over the nations.

To him who overcomes and does My will to the end, I will give authority over the nations—"He will rule them with an iron scepter; he will dash them to pieces like pottery"—just as I have received authority from My Father. I will also give him the morning star.[27]

His authority will be absolute and His edict unequivocal.

Out of His mouth comes a sharp sword with which to strike down the nations. "He will rule them with an iron scepter." He treads the winepress of the fury of the wrath of God Almighty.[28]

The white knight does not destroy the gentile peoples, but He does totally annihilate the beast of the ruling empires. Two things had made dictatorship possible: might and wealth. So the kings of the earth languish over the destruction of the might of the Babylonian system.

When the kings of the earth who committed adultery with her and shared her luxury see the smoke of her burning, they will weep and mourn over her.[29]

And the merchants of the world lament over the destruction of the wealth of the Babylonian style.[30]

What need has Christ for weapons of power? The nuclear arsenals of the world powers mean nothing to the power of the Word of the Almighty. What need has the Creator of the universe for merchandise of gold, silver or pearls, when He builds the foundations of His city on precious stones, garnishes the gates of His city with pearl, and walks on streets of gold?[31] The beast of Babylon has built its kingdom on violence and greed; the Christ of Calvary is building His Kingdom on love and grace. The mountain of brutality and avarice will be crushed by the mountain of compassion and mercy. The beast of falsehood and malice will be defeated by the sword of truth and devotion. Unrighteous kings may ride over the beastly kingdoms of this world, and false prophets, dressed in holy attire, may ride as lords over a subjected humanity, but only One can ride on the steed of moral purity and holiness. The white horse of righteousness and virtue is the horse of victory. Only

the One who can ride the horse of victory can reign.
The kingdoms of the world will fall to the Kingdom of
God. It is the Son of God—Jesus the Christ—who rides
the white horse, and He is the "King of Kings, and Lord
of Lords"![32]

End Notes

1. Dan. 2:31-33. **2.** Dan. 7:2-7. **3.** Dan. 2:44-45. **4.** Dan. 2:42. **5.** Rev. 17:9. **6.** Ps. 30:7. **7.** Jer. 51:25. **8.** Dan. 2:45. **9.** Rev. 17:10. **10.** Rev. 17:12-14. **11.** Ezek. 38. **12.** Dan. 2:44-45. **13.** Rev. 17:4-5 (NIV). **14.** Ex. 34:15-16; Hos. 1:2. **15.** Gen. 11:1-9. **16.** Jer. 25:8-11; Acts 7:43. **17.** Acts 17:23. **18.** John 8:3-11. **19.** Dan. 2:44-45. **20.** Ibid. **21.** Matt. 3:2. **22.** Matt. 4:17. **23.** Matt. 4:23. **24.** Matt. 6:10. **25.** Rom. 14:17. **26.** Rom. 15:12. **27.** Rev. 2:26-28 (NIV). **28.** Rev. 19:15 (NIV). **29.** Rev. 18:9 (NIV). **30.** Rev. 18:11-19. **31.** Rev. 21:18-21. **32.** Rev. 19:16.

Portrait 13

The Alpha and Omega*

The next portrait seems to be an endless living thing. It looks as if the artist placed his brush on the canvas and began to apply his paint in a circular motion, and bits of pigment broke off onto the canvas as his brush moved. That circular motion forms a pattern that appears as the vortex of a whirlwind. Streaks of light and dark blend together, but they are always linked to the original circular motion of the brush. Yet, where the pigments had broken off, patterns of coloring appear.

At the top of the vortex are bits of bright shining pigment that look, to the viewer to be swirling stars and

---

*   Rev. 21:6.

galaxies moving in the blackness of space. Just below, but still centered, is a dark area that has twisting brush strokes, like the texture of wool from a black lamb. To one side of the artist's sweep, a large lump of charcoal pigment has broken off to form the general shape of a mountain, and a similar glob of color has formed a matching shape on the other side of the canvas. As the artist's hand swept downward, the stroke lost some of its circular motion and the vortex became elongated. The texture and coloring of the pigment released from the brush delineates the rough terrain of a wilderness. The texture intensifies as the brush began its upward stroke and repeated a similar process on the other side of the canvas.

Two fiery red balls of paint have seemingly dropped in exact proportions between the mountain, like two lumps. Between the red balls is a crooked, protruding line that stops at what looks like the entrance to a cave. Throughout the vortex on the canvas, one can see etchings depicting the events of time.

When the viewer takes a very close look at the canvas, it is determined that, indeed, the bright lights at its top and center are all of the stars and galaxies. They appear as only small specks of pigment in comparison to the vastness of the painting itself. The black, wool-like strokes are painted as an illustration of chaos. The globs of pigment that broke off to each side are seen, upon close inspection, to indeed depict mountains. The first in the sweep of the vortex is Mount Sinai and the opposite is Mount Zion.

The bright red light near Sinai came from a burning bush that was not consumed and from the light of glory that shone on the face of Moses. The bright red light near Zion came from a fire outside the judgment hall and from the glory that shone on the face of Jesus when He was exalted on the mount of transfiguration.

The elongated portion of the portrait is, indeed, a wilderness. It is the wilderness through which Israel wandered and the wilderness of sin, through which all mankind travels.

The protruding lines in the center of the vortex prove, upon close examination, to be a hill, and the cave holes in it form the outline of a skull. The artist has included the hill of Calvary within the vortex of time!

Swirling from Calvary, in the vortex, are pictured all of the events of time. Satan's rebellion from Heaven is revealed in the black, wool-like strokes of the void. Adam's fall is portrayed, as well as Abraham's sacrifice. Moses and the deliverance of the children of Israel are in the painting, along with Israel's wars to recapture the promised land. All of the wars and violence of history, as well as all of the success and beauty of man, are represented within the sweeping movement of the artist's brush. The most ancient of times and the most modern of times, the creation and the end of creation, the sin and the glory, are all painted in this whirlpool of time.

By backing away from the painting, the viewer is presented with another portrait within the painting. Seen from a distance, the stars at the top of the painting become a diadem of glory. The black wool of chaos becomes a crown of thorns. The mountains of Sinai and Zion become ears framing a head. The wilderness appears as the torn flesh from which His beard was plucked. The burning bush and glory of Moses, as well as the glory of His transfiguration and the fires outside His judgment hall, appear as His saddened eyes. The curvature of His nose in the painting emerges as His bent legs on the cross and the caves of calvary become His nostrils, from which come the breath of life. The painting of the vortex of time is also the face of the savior.

You did not expect to see such a modern, impressionist painting coming from the first Christian century, did you? You will find the explanation on the simple brass plaquette hanging beneath the portrait. The painting is always modern. On the plaquette are engraved two simple Greek characters—Alpha and Omega!

The Christ Before Time

John has painted time. Time begins with the creation of movement from light into darkness and from darkness into light.[1] Existence began before time began.[2] God, who is light and who has no darkness within Himself, created from His own existence.[3] Therefore, when an empty darkness that was without structure came on the earth, it could not have come from God.[4] The apostle Peter wrote:

But they deliberately forget that long ago by God's word the heavens existed and the earth was formed out of water and by water. By these waters also the world of that time was deluged and destroyed. By the same word the present heavens and earth are reserved for fire, being kept for the day of judgment and destruction of ungodly men.[5]

Peter could not have been writing about the flood of Noah, for the entire earth was not destroyed at that time. The context of Peter's remarks are within the scope of the creation. Peter was referring to the destruction indicated in Genesis 1:2. Satan was already in the earth when God made the garden, for he is the dark prince of this world. Jesus existed before the earth, for He is the Light of the world.[6]

John wrote concerning Jesus:

In the beginning was the Word, and the Word was with God, and the Word was God. He was with God in the beginning. Through Him all things were made; without Him nothing was made that has been made. In Him was life, and that life was the light of men.[7]

As the "Word," Jesus is the wisdom of God. Solomon, in his Book of Proverbs, depicted Jesus as incarnate wisdom.[8] Jesus, speaking to the Jews about their father Abraham, said:

Your father Abraham rejoiced at the thought of seeing My day; he saw it and was glad.[9]

Paul wrote of the pre-existing Jesus:

He is the image of the invisible God, the firstborn over all creation. For by Him all things were created: things in heaven and on earth, visible and invisible, whether thrones or powers or rulers or authorities; all things were created by Him and for Him. He is before all things, and in Him all things hold together.[10]

The Cross as the Center of Time

Jesus was born in the "fulness of the time."[11] He was born in the correct place and time, when the conditions for His crucifixion were prepared. He is the "Lamb slain from the foundation of the world."[12] Man did not decide His death. He was crucified by His own will and with foreknowledge of what was to happen.[13] Calvary is in the center of God's purpose, and is the axis upon which time revolves.

Calvary is located theologically between the mountains of Sinai and Jerusalem on Zion. Sinai is where Moses received the Ten Commandments, and it concerns the law and judgment. Zion is where the temple sacrifices were made, and represents grace and forgiveness.[14] Since "all have sinned, and come short of the glory of God" and all, therefore, are judged guilty by the law, the penalty of the law had to be paid.[15] Jesus paid that price through His death on Calvary, thus opening the way to Zion and to God's forgiveness. As the birth of Jesus separates the calendar into B.C. and

A.D., His death separates all time into "under law" and "after grace."

Calvary is not only the axis of universal time, it is also the rod upon which nations and empires will be judged. Because of Christ's death on Calvary, He has the authority to judge all other authorities. In His resurrection power He said, "All authority in heaven and on earth has been given to Me."[16] He has a right to destroy the beast of world empire systems. He gained that right on the cross!

Calvary is also the focal point of individual salvation. The prophet Isaiah described Jesus on the cross:

Just as there were many who were appalled at Him—His appearance was so disfigured beyond that of any man and His form marred beyond human likeness.[17]

He grew up before Him like a tender shoot, and like a root out of dry ground. He had no beauty or majesty to attract us to Him, nothing in His appearance that we should desire Him. He was despised and rejected by men, a man of sorrows, and familiar with suffering. Like one from whom men hid their faces He was despised, and we esteemed Him not. Surely He took up our infirmities and carried our sorrows, yet we considered Him stricken by God, smitten by Him, and afflicted. But He was pierced for our transgressions, He was crushed for our iniquities; the punishment that brought us peace was upon Him, and by His wounds we are healed. We all, like sheep, have gone astray, each of us has turned to his own way; and the Lord has laid on Him the iniquity of us all.[18]

It is from His nail-pierced hands, hanging open on the cross, that individual salvation comes. When an individual comes to the cross, he comes from Mount Sinai—the law. If one has received the blessing of His outstretched arms, he leaves by Mount Zion—grace!

It is from His cross on Calvary that the breath of eternal life comes.[19] The vortex of time is created within the rotation of eternity. As the flow of time moved toward the cross, it was Alpha, the beginning. As the current of time left the cross, it became Omega, the end. The stream of time is created in Him, and the rush of time emanates from him. The Christ of the Apocalypse is time itself—He is Alpha and Omega!

End Notes

1. Gen. 1:4-5. 2. Gen. 1:1. 3. I John 1:5. 4. Gen. 1:2. 5. 2 Pet. 3:5-7 (NIV). 6. John 8:12. 7. John 1:1-4 (NIV). 8. Prov. 8:22-36. 9. John 8:56 (NIV). 10. Col. 1:15-17 (NIV). 11. Gal. 4:4. 12. Rev. 13:8. 13. John 10:17. 14. Gal. 4:25-26. 15. Rom. 3:23. 16. Matt. 28:18 (NIV). 17. Is. 52:14 (NIV). 18. Is. 53:2-6 (NIV). 19. John 3:15.

Portrait 14

The Light of the City*

As a twentieth century visitor to the art gallery of revelation, you will be startled by the next depiction in the archive of the Apocalypse. This painting depicts a scene that could come only from the twenty-first century or beyond, and yet it was first exhibited within the spirit of the apostle John in the first century. It is a painting of modern art and technology that could be classified only as twentieth century science fiction. The scope of the artist's concept exceeds that of the *Star Trek* films or *Space Odyssey 2001*. The painting is a mural upon which a large space station is revealed circling in a fixed orbit above the nation of Israel.

---

*   Rev. 21:10-26.

The space station is of enormous size, and has an unusual shape for an orbiting mass. From north to south, the satellite covers an area of earth including all of the Mediterranean coast, from Spain to Egypt. From east to west, the satellite blankets both the deserts of Arabia and the Mediterranean Sea. The spaceship's phenomenal length and width is rivalled by the fact that its structure is elevated in equal proportion. The city is built in the shape of a perfect cube. Its length and breadth and height are all equal.

Viewing the satellite from its side reveals that it is not solid, but consists of layer after layer of dwelling space. You will see that each layer itself, however, is a complete city, with streets, houses and tall buildings. The entire spacecraft is one massive heavenly city called the New Jerusalem!

John then sketched an enormous wall orbiting the city. Twelve breathtaking foundations, each one painted with the color and texture of a different precious jewel, form the base of the wall and the city. The wall is painted with pigments matching the opaque green color of pure jasper, and its 12 gates are painted with a white marled look, which suggests to the viewer that they might be made of pearl.

The artist has seemingly covered the canvas with luminous pigment. The city and its walls are garnished with the brilliant blue of the sapphire, the marbled blue of the chalcedony, the bright green of the emerald, the red and white of the sardonyx, the reddish-yellow of the sardius, the transparent golden beauty of the chrysolite, the sea-green color of the beryl, the transparent yellow-green color of the topaz, the light green of the chrysoprase, the violet of the jacinth, and the deep purple of the amethyst. If that were not enough, the artist has painted all of the buildings, structures and streets of the city with a paint made from pure gold!

The sky in which the space city orbits appears to be normal. The blue of the heavens frame the space object with a wisp of cloud between it and the earthly Jerusalem. In the sky above the space city, the sun is seen as it travels in its daily flight across the heavens. The sun, however, seems to have lost its brilliance in comparison to the light that comes from the city itself.

I suggest that you guard your eyes when you look directly at the painting. There is such a radiant light streaming from the city that neither the painting nor the room of the gallery in which it hangs has need of any other illumination. The painting shows no source for this marvelous luminosity. You would expect, in such a futuristic concept, that the artist would indicate a nuclear power source, space rays or laser beams lighting the city. Yet the agent for the brilliance of the city appears, in the painting, to be internal to the city itself.

Multitudes of peoples from all nationalities are painted on the earth beneath the city in the portrait. You will recognize kings from their attire and their crowns. The rulers, with all the nations, are portrayed in positions and attitudes of worship and praise. The attention of the worshipers is concentrated on the brilliance of the light radiating out from the city. Now you will be able to see the source of the light. In the reflection in the eyes of the worshipers, the artist has defined the source of the illumination. Each eye mirrors a Lamb made of pure light!

The dazzling uncreated radiant Light of the city is the brightness of God's glory—the Christ of the Apocalypse!

The New Jerusalem

John stood, in the spirit, on a "great and high mountain" and there he viewed the New Jerusalem descending from space like a huge space station. An angel measured the city for John, and it turned out to be 1,500 miles from north to south, 1,500 miles from east to west, and 1,500 miles from top to bottom. The number of levels in the city are not indicated in the painting, but each level is 2,250,000 square miles, covered in pure gold, and rising within the city for 1,500 miles. Since the Scripture is so precise in describing the size of the city and its measurements, it must be concluded that while the language is apocalyptic, the existence and size of the city is not. The shape of the city is a perfect cube. The only other object in the Scriptures described with such detail and in the same shape is the Holy of Holies. The city is the new Holy of Holies![1]

The city will be stationed over Palestine, but if it were placed over the United States, its longitude would cover the entire nation between the borders of Canada and the Gulf of Mexico.

The wall that surrounds the city is not for protection but to indicate, by its open gates, its accessibility. The wall itself measures 216 feet high, which is the height of a 22-story skyscraper. The wall is made from the jasper stone, which has an opaque green coloring. Twelve breathtaking foundations support the wall. Each foundation is made from a differently colored precious jewel, and each foundation is embellished with jewels from the other foundations. The stones pictured in the portrait are exactly the 12 stones of the zodiac:

> amethyst—the Ram;
> jacinth—the Bull;
> chrysoprase—the Twins;
> topaz—the Crab;
> beryl—the Lion;
> chrysolite—the Virgin;
> carnelian—the Balance;
> sardonyx—the Scorpion;
> emerald—the Archer;
> chalcedony—the Goat;
> sapphire—the Water-carrier;
> and jasper—the fishes.

John's revelation, however, lists the stones in precisely their reverse order. The city of the gods of the zodiac is reversed by God's Word. In the world system, and in the supernatural of the occult, knowledge and power is right. In the Kingdom of God, right is knowledge and power! With God, the physical is only a reflection of the spiritual. The creation is only a copy of the eternal. Man is created in the image of his Creator. The occult creates God in the image of man. The image of religion appears to be true, but its right is left and its truth is false.

The word "horoscope" comes from a Latin source that means "to see." Believers in horoscopes think they can forecast events and determine destinies from the positions of the planets and zodiacal signs. This belief started in Babylon as the religion of Zoroastrianism. It is part of the cursed Babylonian system.[2]

The city of Babylon is seen in the Apocalypse, like the New Jerusalem, as being "decked with gold, and precious stones, and pearls!"[3] Babylon is covered with gold, precious stones and pearls because its residents are attempting to imitate the true city of God. The order of its foundations, however, reveal it to be only a reflection; the New Jerusalem is the true city of God!

There are 12 gates in the wall. Each gate is made from a single pearl. In John's time, the pearl was the most valuable of all jewels. A merchant would sell all that he had for the perfect pearl.[4] The gates of pearl tell the visitor to the city that within it are unmeasurable riches. The gates themselves are grandiose. To correctly fit a wall that extends 1,500 miles, they have to be enormous in size.

The city is the abode of God the Father, God the son, God the Holy Spirit, and the Bride. Beneath the orbiting city, the earth is in full blossom and productivity. The earth is populated by the "nations." These are righteous people who live in mortal bodies as did Adam and Eve before the fall of man, the natural seed of Abraham in their mortal bodies, and the Church.[4] They travel between the earth and the New Jerusalem as administrators of the earth.[5]

For all the size and splendor of the mural, the size, gold, and luster of the wall and city would have no meaning if it were not for the brilliant blaze of light that radiates from it. The elucidating power of the city is produced by the glory coming from a Lamb.

The Light of the Word

John saw "no temple" in the city[6] The universe had become the temple, in the painting, and the city itself the Holy of Holies. From the ancient Holy of Holies in the temple came the *shekinah* light of God. This was the same glory that led the children of Israel as a pillar of cloud and fire. This is the glory of the Lord as seen by the prophet Isaiah when he wrote:

Arise, shine, for your light has come, and the glory of the Lord rises upon you. See, darkness covers the earth and thick darkness is over the peoples, but the Lord rises upon you and His glory appears over you. Nations will come to your light, and kings to the brightness of your dawn.[7]

Both Isaiah's revelation and John's portrait concern Christ's administration over the earth during the millennium.[8] His dominion is always one of light that shines against the darkness of error and sin. John is told, concerning the city:

Nothing impure will ever enter it, nor will anyone who does what is shameful or deceitful, but only those whose names are written in the Lamb's book of life.[9]

Deceit cannot exist in the pure light of truth! Jesus is the light of truth that came to shine in the world of darkness and falsehood.[10]

Death cannot exist in the presence of the Lamb, "who has destroyed death and has brought life and immortality to light through the gospel."[11] Only those who have received Jesus Christ as their Light become children of the Light and enter the Holy City whose Light is the Lamb.[12] The source of the light in the New Jerusalem is a Lamb because it is by the slain Lamb of God on the cross that eternal darkness and death was defeated. It was as the Lamb that Jesus was placed into the dark tomb of death, and as the Lamb He was resurrected. The power that raised the Lamb from the dead is the energy of the Light of the City. Jesus, the Lamb, is "declared to be the Son of God with power, according to the spirit of holiness, by the resurrection from the dead."[13]

The brightness of the light of the resurrection is greater than any power known to man. No nuclear fusion could produce enough energy and light to bring even one dead person to life, yet the resurrection power in Jesus is strong enough to open the graves of all men born since the creation. The resurrection power in the Lamb is potent enough to create a new heaven and a new earth in which the newly resurrected mankind can live. The resurrection power in the Christ is dynamic enough to brilliantly light the New Jerusalem. The resurrection power of the Light is radiant enough to illuminate all of the millennial world. The resurrection power of Jesus is sufficient to flow out of the frame of the painting, into the gallery, through the archive of the Apocalypse, and into the soul of the viewer, turning sin into righteousness and the darkness of death into the light of eternal life!

End Notes

1. Rev. 21:10-23. **2.** Rev. 18:2. **3.** Rev. 18:16. **4.** Matt. 13:46. **5.** Ezek. 36:11. **6.** Rev. 21:22. **7.** Is. 60:1-3 (NIV). **8.** Rev. 19:15. **9.** Rev. 21:27 (NIV). **10.** John 1:4. **11.** 2 Tim. 1:10 (NIV). **12.** Rev. 21:23. **13.** Rom. 1:4.

Portrait 15

The River of Life[*]

Our next painting is a landscape. Water tumbles from an infinity of sky into a crystal clear river. At the base of the waterfall, the river swirls and churns white with froth in the shallows. As the banks of the river rise and the river deepens, you can see that the surface of the water calms. Like a mirror, the artist paints on the river's surface the scenic vista through which it flows.

The shores of the river are blanketed with green, grassy slopes. Trees line its banks. The dark green leaves of the trees accentuate the fact that each tree is bearing 12 different kinds of brightly colored fruit. See, on the surface of the river, the artist has painted the reflection of the multicolored and differently shaped

---

* Rev. 22:1-7.

fruit. A thin line of gold divides the reflection of the fruit and trees from the bank of the river. Notice that the golden line is itself a reflection of two streets of pure gold that border the river on each side. As the sketch of the river crosses the canvas, the river becomes wider and deeper. Ripples in the reflections along its banks indicate that the current is increasing with the river's length. The surge of water depicted indicates that a flood is moving quickly toward the frame of the painting. Then the landscape ends suddenly, even before it fills the frame. It is almost as if the artist had run out of paint. The picture disappears into a void of untouched canvas. One who traces the flow of the river knows that the water in the painted river would, should the artist complete the landscape, flow over the frame. But, because the artist left the canvas unfinished, the viewer cannot project either the course of the water or the swiftness of its arrival at the frame of infinity. This is a landscape, yet the entire painting is an apocalyptic portrait of Jesus Christ!

The Water

During the Jewish festival of Tabernacles, a priest took a golden pitcher and filled it with water from the pool of Siloam. He then carried the pitcher of water into the city of Jerusalem through the water gate. As the water was brought into the city, the people recited the words of the prophet Isaiah: "With joy shall ye draw water out of the wells of salvation."[1] When the priest reached the temple and the altar, the water that he had not spilled in the process was poured out as an offering to God.

It was at the moment of the offering of the water that Jesus cried out:

If anyone is thirsty, let him come to Me and drink. Whoever believes in Me, as the Scripture has said, streams of living water will flow from within him.[2]

Jesus was using apocalyptic language to describe Himself as the "fountain" that comes from the house of the Lord.[3] The apostle Paul wrote that Jesus was the rock from which the water of life flowed.[4] The river John saw in the Apocalypse is called "a pure river of water of life;" Jesus said to the woman of Samaria that the water He gave would be living water "springing up into everlasting life."[5]

It is impossible to separate the water from the river. Without water, a river is not a river. Is the water the Holy Spirit?[6] Then Jesus is the river through which the Spirit flows! Is the river the Holy Spirit? Then Jesus is the source of the water! Jesus gives the refreshment of the Holy Spirit! Jesus is the water of life that purifies and fills. Jesus is the source of life for all eternity.

The river increases in depth as it flows out from the throne. Ezekiel wrote of the river flowing from the throne of God:

He then brought me out through the north gate and led me around the outside to the outer gate facing east, and the water was flowing from the south side.

As the man went eastward with a measuring line in his hand, he measured off a thousand cubits and then led me through water that was ankle-deep. He measured off another thousand cubits and led me through water that was knee-deep. He measured off another thousand and led me through water that was up to the waist. He measured off another thousand, but now it was a river that I could not cross, because the water had risen and was deep enough to swim in—a river that no one could cross. He asked me, "Son of man, do you see this?"

Then he led me back to the bank of the river. When I arrived there, I saw a great number of trees on each side of the river. He said to me, "This water flows toward the eastern region and goes down into the Arabah, where it enters the Sea. When it empties into the Sea, the water there becomes fresh. Swarms of living creatures will live wherever the river flows. There will be large numbers of fish, because this water flows there and makes the salt water fresh; so where the river flows everything will live. Fishermen will stand along the shore; from En Gedi to En Eglaim there will be places for spreading nets. The fish will be of many kinds—like the fish of the Great Sea. But the swamps and marshes will not become fresh; they will be left for salt. Fruit trees of all kinds will grow on both banks of the river. Their leaves will not wither, nor will their fruit fail. Every month they will bear, because the water from the sanctuary flows to them. Their fruit will serve for food and their leaves for healing."[7]

Like the landscape in John's portrait, Ezekiel saw the river flowing from the city of God. Ezekiel's vision and John's apocalypse are similar in that both see the source of the river within the city, trees on each side of the river, 12 types of fruit (bearing each month), and healing leaves. Ezekiel's man with the measuring line, however, disclosed that the river deepened the further it flowed from the source. The Word of God deepens as it flows from the Book of Genesis to the Book of the Revelation. His Word is built.

For precept must be upon precept, precept upon precept, line upon line, line upon line; here a little, and there a little.[8]

The Holy Spirit is to become such a river that it overflows from the life of the believer.

He that believeth on Me, as the scripture hath said, out of his belly shall flow rivers of living water.[9]

Jesus Christ is the living water that supplies all the grace needed to produce life and growth on both sides of Calvary. From the temple of God, His body on Calvary, the river of life flows![10]

The Tree

The tree of life and the tree of the knowledge of good and evil first grew in the garden of Eden.[11] God commanded only that the parents of the human race not take of the tree of the knowledge of good and evil.[12] Both the trees were apocalyptic in nature. The fruit of the tree of the knowledge of good and evil was death.[13] Jesus has life within Himself.

For as the Father has life in Himself, so He has granted the Son to have life in Himself.[14]

Jesus answered, "I am the way and the truth and the life. No one comes to the Father except through Me."[15]

The fruit of the tree of life would have produced eternal life.[16] Therefore, the tree of life represented Jesus and the tree of the knowledge of good and evil represented death. To accept the fruit of death is to reject the fruit of life. By receiving the fruit of the tree of the knowledge of good and evil, Adam and Eve placed the hope of a self-affirming validity above the expectations of a God-avowed perfection. The desire for knowledge became greater than the desire for relationship!

The tree of the knowledge of good and evil cannot grow on the bank of the river of life. The cross of Christ meant the death of death. The resurrection of Christ is a resurrection to life. The fruit of the knowledge of good and evil is the fruit of sin and death. The fruit of the tree of life is the fruit of the Spirit of life.

The tree of life has 12 different kinds of fruit growing from it. There is a tree of life on each side of the river of life. On the pre-Calvary side of the river of life, the fruit represents the 12 patriarchs and thus the 12 tribes of Israel. For the tree on the post-Calvary side of the river, the 12 kinds of fruit represent the apostles of Jesus Christ and the Church. Abraham drank from the river of life by faith, looking toward the cross and the city of God.[17] Paul drank from the river of life by faith, looking backward to the cross and in hope toward the city of God.[18]

The flavor of the fruit comes from the character of the tree (Jesus). Thus, one can expect to find the flavors of love, joy, peace, longsuffering, gentleness, goodness, faith, meekness and temperance, when the fruit is tasted.[19]

Isaiah wrote:

But He was pierced for our transgressions, He was crushed for our iniquities; the punishment that brought us peace was upon Him, and by His wounds we are healed.[20]

The lush leaves of the trees are medicinal. They are "for the healing of the nations."[21] The leaves of the tree of life represent the wounds of Jesus. Leaves cover the tree as stripes covered the body of the Savior. Jeremiah asked, "Is there no balm in Gilead; is there no physician there? why then is not the health of the daughter of my people recovered?"[22] Jeremiah was referring to the medicinal properties of a small evergreen tree and relating it to spiritual healing for Israel. Jesus is the answer to Jeremiah's question. Through the bruising of the Savior, all of the curse has been removed.

He will wipe every tear from their eyes. There will be no more death or mourning or crying or pain, for the old order of things has passed away.[23]

"The healing of the nations" may refer to the physical healing of those who enter the millennial reign in their natural bodies, while the saints are in spiritual bodies.[24] Or, it could be an apocalyptic image. the leaves of the tree of life are similar to His stripes in that they are publicly displayed. The leaves are analogous to His wounds, in that balm is produced in the crushing. For the Church, in natural or spiritual bodies, the truth is the same: "With His stripes we are healed."[25]

The Unfinished Canvas

History is an account of the events that occur along the banks of the river of life. All of history is divided by the water that flowed from Jesus' side as He hung on the cross. The events of life flow steadily with the current. History is not an accident, nor does it lack direction. The river of life flows toward the frame of infinity, but the artist has deliberately left some of the mural unfinished. It is not that the artist is uncertain about the course of the river or of the swiftness of the flow of the water. The painting is completed in his mind, but his hand stays the brush. What if the viewer is unprepared for the river in the canvas becoming a torrent, flowing over the frame into the gallery?

Jesus warns:

Behold, I am coming soon! Blessed is he who keeps the words of the prophecy in this book.[26]

Behold, I am coming soon! My reward is with Me, and I will give to everyone according to what he has done.[27]

No man knows the procession of the climax of history. Jesus said that information was reserved for His Father.[28] The river of life continues its flow across the canvas. In a moment of time, a brush stroke will complete the painting. A mighty torrent of life will flow into eternity. The river of life will overflow its banks and pour over the frame of the portrait to engulf totality. The Christ of the Apocalypse will fill all eternity, for He—Jesus Christ—is eternal life!

End Notes

1. Isa. 12:3. **2.** John 7:37-38. **3.** Joel 3:18. **4.** I Cor. 10:4. **5.** John 4:14. **6.** John 7:38-39. **7.** Ezek. 47:2-12 (NIV). **8.** Isa. 28:10. **9.** John 7:38. **10.** John 2:21; John 19:34. **11.** Gen. 2:9. **12.** Gen. 2:17. **13.** Ibid. **14.** John 5:26 (NIV). **15.** John 14:6 (NIV). **16.** Gen. 3:22. **17.** Heb. 11:10. **18.** Rom. 4:13-25. **19.** Gal. 5:22-23. **20.** Isa. 53:5. **21.** Rev. 22:2. **22.** Jer. 8:22. **23.** Rev. 21:4. **24.** I Cor. 15:44. **25.** Isa. 53:5. **26.** Rev. 22:7 (NIV). **27.** Rev. 22:12 (NIV). **28.** Acts 1:7.

The Mezzanine

We have been walking through an art gallery, the archive of the spirit of John the Revelator. The gallery has many exhibits, but we have chosen to view only that section in which the portraits of Christ of the Apocalypse are displayed. The handbook has attempted to point out various details and the significance of each painting. The fact that the guide is interpretative has been clearly recognized. Now you are invited to walk back through the gallery at your own pace.

Study again the perceptions John had of Christ. Look deeply into the face of the Christ of the Apocalypse. Examine for yourself the details of the paintings. Observe the pigment and the coloring. Assess the bold or delicate strokes of the brush. Look again at all the details surrounding the portraits.

But be careful what you concentrate on and how you perceive Him! Some look at the apocalypse and see only tribulation, beasts, war, famine, destruction and desolation. Some look at the judgment seat of Christ and tremble with fear, trepidation and despair. Some look into the eyes of Christ of the Apocalypse and see sternness, legalism, judgment, denunciation and disparity. Others look at the Christ of the Apocalypse and see love, hope, and even joy. They recognize the horror portrayed in the tribulation, but through it all they see the comforting arms of a loving God. These viewers find a Christ that can even laugh and celebrate in the midst of darkness. In the dark foreboding colors of judgment, these viewers see bright flashes of light. In the eyes of Christ, some can see all the colors of the rainbow.

The warning to be careful in perceiving Christ of the Apocalypse is given because you will find a mirror on the wall as you leave the gallery. Each time you pass through the mezzanine, be sure to closely examine your reflection in the mirror. Paul wrote:

But we all, with open face beholding as in a glass the glory of the Lord, are changed into the same image from glory to glory, even as by the Spirit of the Lord.[1]

The rewards of the apocalypse are described in terms of golden crowns, treasures, rulership of cities, and streets of pure gold. We must not forget that these are apocalyptic terms. The great gift is Christ Himself! He gives us Himself that we might become like Him.

That is the purpose of the Revelation of John—that we might see Jesus and so become like Him.

John writes that the one who keeps his book will be blessed.[2] That is why this handbook to the art gallery of the Christ of the Apocalypse was written—that you might see Jesus and be blessed.

Now please accept my invitation to examine the mirror again before you leave the gallery!

End Notes

1. II Cor. 3:18. **2.** Rev. 22:7.

A Biblical Epic
in the Tradition of
Ben Hur and *The Robe*

Born to Triumph

Adventure! Intrigue! Betrayal! Love! Set in the dynamic conflict between Rome and Jerusalem, C. Paul Willis portrays the apostle Paul as a dynamic Roman born to power who is also a Jew born to principles. The struggle between sin, law and grace are fought out between the apostle's two natures, the women in his life, and in his very soul. This sweeping adventure moves the reader from the halls of power in Rome to the nefarious corruption of the temple, the stark reality of Calvary, the Church in conflict, and finally to the triumph of grace.

Born to Triumph is available from Christian Word Books, 4501 Lake Jeanette Rd., Greensboro, NC 27455; Destiny Image Publishers; or your favorite bookstore.

Bells & Pomegranates

There are nine gifts of the Spirit and nine fruit of the Spirit found in the New Testament. Dr. C. Paul Willis believes that the gifts and fruit are interrelated. Gifts are given, but fruit must be developed. In *Bells & Pomegranates,* Willis explains how the gifts of the Spirit are to be used in the church and how the fruit of the Spirit are to be developed. He clarifies the interrelationship between gifts and fruit and illustrates the union through the bells and pomegranates that hung from the robe of the high priest of Israel.

Bells & Pomegranates is available from Christian Word Books, 4501 Lake Jeanette Rd., Greensboro, NC 27455; Destiny Image Publishers; or your favorite bookstore.